Educating Your Child at Home

Also available in the series

Richard Andrews: *Teaching and Learning English*
John Ecclestone (ed.): *Teaching and Learning Design and Technology*
Dawn Hamilton: *Passing Exams*
Gordon Lloyd: *How Exams Really Work*
Marilyn Nickson: *Teaching and Learning Maths*
Alan Thomas: *Educating Children at Home*

EDUCATING YOUR CHILD AT HOME

Jane Lowe and Alan Thomas

continuum
LONDON • NEW YORK

Continuum

The Tower Building   370 Lexington Avenue
11 York Road   New York
London SE1 7NX   NY 10017–6503

www.continuumbooks.com

First published 2002

British Library Cataloguing-in-Publication Data
A catalogue record for this book is available from the British Library.

ISBN 0–8264–5227–2 (paperback)

Typeset by YHT Ltd, London
Printed and bound in Great Britain by Biddles Ltd, Guildford and King's Lynn

Contents

	Preface	vii
CHAPTER 1	Thinking about home education	1
CHAPTER 2	Learning at home is not like learning in school	8
CHAPTER 3	Informal learning	20
CHAPTER 4	Starting out	38
CHAPTER 5	Learning at home in the primary years	55
CHAPTER 6	Projects	79
CHAPTER 7	Learning at home in the secondary years	83
CHAPTER 8	Social life	121
CHAPTER 9	Special educational needs	131
CHAPTER 10	Options as children grow older	141
CHAPTER 11	Some final reflections	150
	References	157
	Addresses and further reading	158
	Index	161

Preface

There is little doubt that home education (home schooling in some countries) is a valid and acceptable alternative to school. That is as far as we will go. We are not anti-school. Our intention is not to persuade you to become a home educator. It is simply to inform you about home education. We believe it is important that you should be well-informed, whether you are thinking of giving home education a try from the start when your child reaches school age or if you have a child who is experiencing difficulties in school.

This book should also prove useful for parents who have recently become home educators and are unsure of how to go about it. We don't set out to tell you how to teach your child at home, but our book will have served its purpose if it helps you to find your own way forward.

Your children may be happily enrolled in school and you are simply curious about home education. If so, this book will give you ideas about how to support your children's learning, not just by helping with homework, but also informally during family activities. It will also be something to keep at the back of your mind should you ever need to consider it.

CHAPTER 1

Thinking about home education

Home education: the background

During the past thirty years this richly varied, interesting and in-novative movement has emerged on the education scene, especially in the UK, Ireland, North America and Australasia. Home education, also known as home schooling, has grown from its small beginnings among the rich, the radical and the geographically isolated to become an officially recognized aspect of educational diversity in many countries today. Now almost everyone knows someone who is educating children at home or who has done so in recent years.

Books, magazines, websites, internet groups, support organizations, informal networks and educational resources are readily available. The isolation that was felt by the early pioneers has faded away and there is now a flourishing community which continues to expand rapidly. There is still much to discover about the day-to-day practice of home education but recent research has shown that it may have much to teach us, particularly with regard to individualized teaching and more flexible styles of learning.

Who are the home educators? They come from all social back-grounds and all income levels. There are large families and families with one child; there are also couples and single parents. The main educator is usually the mother but there are also other relatives including grandparents, aunts, uncles and older brothers or sisters who are engaged in the activity of education at home. There are people of every conceivable religious, political and philosophical standpoint. Home educators have all levels of qualifications from none at all to higher degrees. About a quarter of home educators have a teacher in the family, half of whom think that their training is helpful while the other half consider that it gets in the way when they are teaching at home.

How many home educated children are there? In the UK estimates vary wildly between 10,000 and 150,000 or more. There is no research basis whatsoever for these figures. Estimates at the higher end may include children who are out of school for all sorts of reasons, but who should not be counted among children who are receiving education at home by parental choice. A recent feasibility study (Petrie *et al.*, 1999) showed that it would not be possible to arrive at anything approaching a reasonable estimate of the numbers involved until a question is included in the National Census. The main reason for this is that children who have never been registered at a school are usually not known to the local education authorities (LEAs). In addition, LEA records are by no means reliable. Also, families who are moving into an area don't have any obligation to notify the education authority of their arrival. A similar situation obtains in many other countries. It's likely that the United States has the highest proportion of home educating families and estimates suggest that there may be a million home schooled children in the USA.

What is known with some certainty, though, is that the number of children who are educated at home is increasing. Home Education Advisory Service (HEAS) and Education Otherwise (EO), the national home education organizations in the UK, both report a growing membership and a steady increase in the number of enquiries received from parents.

Why are parents choosing this form of education for their children in preference to school? Some families decide on home education before their children reach school age, but others turn to it after a crisis in school. Parents who decide to educate their children at home from the beginning are usually well informed about it, having done much reading and thinking during the pre-school years. They may have seen that their child is already learning a great deal at home and this leads them to want to continue the process. They may feel that their child is not ready to start school and they may decide to continue at home for a couple of years. There are some who educate at home who believe that the moral values of schools are unacceptable, usually for religious reasons. There are libertarian parents who believe that education should not be coercive and that their children should be in control of their own education. Others are concerned about educational standards in schools; some can't afford private education; some fail to get a place for their child at the school of their choice. These are some of the most common reasons why increasing numbers of parents are choosing to take their own path outside the school system, but there are many others.

Parents who decide to withdraw their child from school often do so in a hurry. Sometimes a crisis may occur after years of misery in school, and there is a need to act quickly. In these cases parents may not have the luxury of preparing for home education in advance. Bullying is the reason which parents cite most often when they withdraw a child from school; in most cases the children are victims but in a few instances they are the perpetrators of it. In a few cases children have talked of committing suicide and others have attempted it. Some children are deeply unhappy in school and this leads to health problems and school phobia. Sometimes children with special educational needs have difficulties in a mainstream setting, and this may lead to acute problems.

In other instances withdrawal from school may be a way of managing a situation where a child is failing academically; some children may be falling behind while others are streets ahead and insufficiently challenged. A few children find out about home education for themselves and ask their parents to give it a try.

Regardless of the reason why they began in the first place, home educators everywhere have shown for years that learning at home is a viable option. We can say with some certainty based on a great deal of experience that we have come across hardly anyone who has regretted having educated children at home, whether in the short or in the long term. It might be useful to bear in mind that if you do decide to educate your children at home, it doesn't mean that you are committed to your decision all the way through until they reach the age of 16. As long as a suitable school place is available, there is nothing to prevent them from attending school at some time in the future.

If your child has never been to school ...

Teaching your child at home may be a continuation of the learning experience of the pre-school years. Remember that the parent is the first educator of the child. In the past, basic education, consisting mainly of literacy and numeracy, was nearly always carried out informally at home by parents who would never have thought of themselves as teachers. This principle still holds good today and the only difference is that the emphases have changed. In addition to literacy and numeracy young children learn to operate computers, telephones, videos and a range of everyday technology in the home. They also have much more information available to them than did our predecessors. Experienced home educators will tell you that they see no reason why a child's learning environment should need to change overnight simply because their offspring have reached the age of 5. Why send your children to school when they are learning perfectly well at home?

Life will be different, of course, if you decide to go ahead with home education. You will have doubts and fears as well as a sense of great adventure at the thought of sharing in your children's learning. You will have to share your living space with paintings, models, puppets, washing-soda stalactites on the windowsill, wormeries and cardboard spaceships. There will be books and other paraphernalia everywhere and, although you never seem to be able to find them, lots of overdue library books. Your child will want to talk to you, and talk to you, and talk to you. You will find yourself constantly responding to 'Not in school today?' as you go to the supermarket and the park. Some friends may suddenly start avoiding you in case your offspring infect their children with the dangerous idea that they don't have to go to school! You will be ferrying your children around a great deal to make sure they have adequate contact with other children. You will get to know all your local amenities, libraries, museums and parks especially and all the people working in them. Most of all, if it's a nice day you can just go out and enjoy it.

What will happen as the children grow older? Parents often say that the secret of successful home education is to relax into your role as educator and grow with your children. As the work becomes more wide-ranging, you will be able to learn together. Take each stage as it comes and your confidence will increase as you realize that you can help your children to learn.

... and if you are withdrawing your child from school

Many parents find that they are forced to begin home education when there are serious problems at school. Sometimes there's no other way of safeguarding the child's physical and mental health apart from removal from the situation and educating the child at home. Problems at school may occur at any age and parents may find themselves in charge of their child's education overnight if there is a crisis. Can home education be successful in these circumstances?

Clearly it's easier and less stressful if you have had the opportunity to plan a child's withdrawal from school but it's not essential. The local education authority will probably ask you for information about your arrangements when you have had time to get organized, but you are entitled to a reasonable amount of time in which to set up the education at home.

When a child has been withdrawn as a result of trauma and unhappiness at school it's nearly always the case that a period of adjustment is needed before education can get under way. Children who have spent years in school may take some time to adapt to the new situation at home, and if they have lost their faith in themselves they may need time to recover. Motivation to learn is damaged when a child has been bullied or when a child has failed in school; others may have lost interest if their experience of school was not sufficiently challenging.

Be prepared to be flexible, patient, calm and adaptable during this initial phase of recovery, which may last for quite a long time. It's not necessary to follow a set course of study but it's wise to keep your own record of the education that you are providing. The experience of many home educators confirms that it may be a big mistake to spend large amounts of money on expensive resources at an early stage. You and your child will both need time to settle in to home education and you will need to decide on the kind of arrangement that will suit your own situation. Some families start by imitating school at home while others begin by getting as far away as possible from anything that is associated with school.

The first few weeks and months may be difficult and challenging for both child and parent, especially when the initial sense of relief has evaporated. It may help to remember that very many home educating families have been there too, and they have survived. Bear in mind that it's not necessary to be an expert in order to help your child to learn. Academic and professional qualifications are not relevant at home. Commitment, time and a willingness to learn yourself are far more important than teaching experience, together with the desire to be actively involved in helping your child to learn. It also helps enormously to relax and to have a sense of fun.

The legality of home education

Nowadays, the chances of a home educator coming up against the law are remote. So we'll be very brief, restricting ourselves to what you might want to know if you're asked about it by relatives, neighbours or friends. Unless the legal situation changes, it should not really influence your decision to home educate. The focus of this book is educational, therefore what follows is simply a brief outline of the main points of the law. Once you have decided to go ahead with home education we recommend that you join one of the national home education organizations for further details.

In the UK, education is compulsory but school is not. The responsibility for providing education lies with the parents and this duty is fulfilled by ensuring that the child is educated either by regular attendance at school or otherwise.

But be aware, should you move out of England or Wales, that the situation varies from country to country, including Scotland and Ireland. Home education is legal in most countries and expatriate families can often continue with home education even in places where it is not officially recognized. The national organizations should be able to give

up-to-date advice and information about the legality of home education in other parts of the world.

If you live in the UK there is no legal obligation to inform anyone,
including the local education authority (LEA), if your child does not
start school on reaching the age of 5, though some parents prefer to tell
the LEA about their decision. If you withdraw a child from a mainstream school in England and Wales the only requirement is simply to
inform the school in writing of your decision. The school must notify
the LEA within two weeks of receiving your letter. The LEA will
probably ask for information about the home education but they must
wait for a reasonable amount of time so that the parents may set up
their arrangements. Most families allow the LEA's representative to
visit them informally at home but some prefer to meet elsewhere or to
provide a report and evidence in writing. Our conversations with
parents indicate that in most cases their relationships with the LEA are
satisfactory. In some areas there may be problems, and usually these
are due to a lack of understanding of the law on the part of the LEA's
representative.

UK law requires that the education which is to be provided must be
'efficient', 'full-time' and 'suitable' to the child's 'age, ability and ap-
titude and to any special educational needs' that he or she may have.
All these terms with the exception of the last are not defined in law
and are therefore open to interpretation. Home educators need not
follow the national curriculum and they do not have to submit their
child for national tests. Education at home may be full-time without
taking up the same amount of time as a school day, and school terms
do not apply at home.

In England and Wales part-time schooling is permitted in law but
successful arrangements with maintained schools are rare. A part-time
schooling arrangement is made at the discretion of the school and it is
not classed as home education. The child is registered as a pupil at the
school and given leave of absence for part of the time in order to be
'educated off site' as it is recorded in the school register. The education
has to conform to the national curriculum if the child attends on a
part-time basis at a maintained school.

On home ground

Home educators do have some significant advantages in comparison
with school. Your child is able to benefit from one-to-one teaching and
the flexibility that goes with learning at home. These advantages
cannot be provided by a teacher in a classroom and home educating
parents generally find that they more than make up for any lack of
qualifications. This is not a criticism of the teaching profession, be-

cause teachers have to acquire the very difficult skill of trying to advance the learning of around thirty children of different abilities. The children in the classroom may all have different levels of motivation and different rates of learning, but the teacher has to teach them all at the same time!

To take sole responsibility for their children's learning might seem to be a daunting task at first, but most parents find home education highly rewarding once they have established themselves. It's important to be well informed, and we hope that the experience of many families which is included in the following chapters will provide both information and reassurance.

CHAPTER 2

Learning at home is not like learning in school

Differences between home and school

Learning at home nearly always turns out to be very different from the experience of learning in school. It's natural, though, that parents and others who aren't familiar with home education nearly always think of it at first as school at home.

We are all products of our own education and it can be surprisingly difficult to envisage anything that is radically different from our own experience. Many years ago when one of us, Jane, was an English teacher at a secondary school she remembers using an extract from a course book which was about a boy who was educated at home. She discussed it with her Year 7 class and they talked about what home education would be like. But when they were asked to write about what they would do if they had the freedom to learn anything they wished at home, everyone came up with a daily routine of half-hour lessons in all their normal school subjects!

In the same way, many parents start out with the assumption that it must be necessary to replicate school at home in order to make a success of home education. But the concept of home education differs fundamentally from the school model in a number of ways. Table 2.1 gives a summary of the most significant differences which apply at least until the beginning of GCSE, and these are discussed in more detail below.

Qualifications

Teachers in school must be qualified to teach, but parents who educate their children at home do not need to have teaching qualifications. People tend to assume that parents must possess the knowledge and expertise of at least ten teachers in order to provide a good education at home for their child, but this is not necessary. In fact, home educators who are also teachers often say that their professional training is not relevant because the task of teaching large groups of pupils in

In school	At home
Teachers are qualified	No qualifications are needed
The national curriculum is obligatory	The national curriculum does not apply at home
Detailed long-term planning is needed	Detailed planning is not necessary; parents may change and adapt as they go along
Lessons are timetabled	Timetables are not necessary
Teachers must have a very good grasp of the content of each lesson beforehand	This is not required; parents may learn alongside their children
Children have lessons all day	Formal learning is usually restricted to an hour or two, often in the morning
There is little informal learning	Informal learning is very important
Children constantly produce written work as evidence of learning and attainment	Written work is far less important; parents generally know what stage their children have reached
Children's work is marked and graded	Marking is unnecessary at home because any mistakes or difficulties are dealt with as they occur
Individualized teaching is very rare	Almost all teaching is individualized
Teachers are trained to teach reading	Training for teaching reading is unnecessary
There is little time for reading for pleasure	Most children are avid readers
There are opportunities for group learning, including activities such as drama and sport	These opportunities have to be created
Children mix a lot with many others of the same age	Children mix with fewer individuals, but they may socialize with adults and children of all ages

Table 2.1 *Differences between school and home*

school bears little resemblance to teaching one or two children at home. Parents are able to guide their children's learning on an individual basis at home without any specialist subject knowledge, even when they are preparing for GCSE. At this stage some parents may prefer to seek some input from correspondence courses or from tutors, but others carry on by themselves by obtaining the syllabuses and some suitable books and materials. There's more on the subject of exams in Chapter 10.

The national curriculum

The national curriculum decides the content of children's learning in maintained schools, and independent schools also follow it to a large extent. But as we've already seen, the national curriculum is not obligatory at home and there are no compulsory subjects. Parents are free to establish their own philosophy and goals. There is no evidence to support any theory of 'best practice' in home education and parents use a variety of methods and approaches. These range from formal, structured arrangements to informal approaches which are completely child-led. Once they have settled down to learning at home, most home educators seem to evolve their own approach which falls somewhere in the middle between these two extremes. Even when home education takes place in a formal and structured manner it differs greatly from school, and Alan has analysed the interesting reasons behind this difference in his book *Educating Children at Home* in some detail (Thomas, 2000). In a nutshell, we can say that although some home educators might start out with the intention of following the school model at home, they soon discover that learning at home is very different from learning at school.

There's more about the practical implications of the different approaches to home education in Chapter 4.

Planning

At school detailed long-term planning is needed to ensure delivery of the curriculum to all children. If they wish to do so, parents who teach their children at home may dispense with planning altogether in order to adapt to the everchanging nature of learning. We sense when it's time to insist, when to desist and when to try a different tack. There is time to listen to a child to see how a task is conceived or to get a fuller picture of any difficulty in understanding. When we are dealing with children at home we may adjust our teaching to their needs, minute by minute, in a way that is impossible in the classroom. It soon becomes evident that detailed preparation is largely unnecessary at home. You don't have to prepare a lesson to teach a whole class of children. At home, you can simply start from where you left off last time. If you want to, you can get a step ahead as you are settling down together. If you are unsure at some stage you can just take a short break while you work out for yourself how to proceed to the next step. Some families continue to learn in an informal and spontaneous manner well into the secondary years, and planning need not be undertaken at all unless you decide to undertake GCSE at home.

Timetables

Unlike home, timetables are essential in school. Schools are institutions which have little flexibility. The school timetable is a massive and complex affair that often demands the attention of several members of staff for months before the new academic year begins. It is unthinkable for a school to function without one but at home a timetable is not necessary. It's common for families to start off with a timetable which divides each day's work into 'lessons', but this is often abandoned altogether as they settle in to education at home. Other families find that it's useful to follow a timetable for part of the day. Yolande explains that a structured but relaxed approach suited her daughter Becky:

> We try to stick to a schedule, but sometimes you don't, not every day. We start between 10.00 and 10.30 and finish at lunchtime. The rest of the day, we may go to the park or there's art on Monday and dancing on Friday. On Tuesday we go to my mother's. Sometimes we drive to the beach or to the country. We play ball games, go swimming and ice skating. We used to go horseriding. Becky doesn't have any trouble getting her work done. She says that she does a lot more than in school.

At school children have to conform to the timetable and they know that Art will take place on Fridays after morning break every week, for example, for the entire school year. Inspiration, creativity and imagination are needed routinely on Friday mornings whether the child feels so inclined or not. Home education allows for spontaneity in order to foster your child's creativity, as Silvia explains:

> For the first year we were under pressure to have something to show – a set curriculum – something to follow. But since then it's got a lot more lax, instead of having timetables and books and having to achieve a certain amount. It's become more on the quality and if they enjoy doing something. For example, yesterday Chris [aged 11] was going to write poems out when Tony [my partner] said something about making a boat. Chris spent the whole morning on it. If it's flowing like that it's wrong to say 'stop this'. It's a privilege to see it happen like that.

When your child's learning takes place at home you don't have to start or finish at any particular time. The education may take place at the weekend or in the evening if you wish. Sometimes children are tired or unwell or they may be unable to concentrate for a number of reasons, and their learning is ineffective. When there is nothing to be gained from persevering you may break off and come back to the task later. Thus the time spent in learning tends to be profitable and intensive, and this explains why most home educators find that it's not necessary to spend the whole day on formal learning activities.

Another advantage of working in a flexible manner without a rigid timetable is that children may continue with an activity if they are particularly involved with it. Some children become interested in a subject and they will continue to explore it for days or longer. Tracey found that her son learned best if he spent blocks of time on a subject:

> He'd spend a whole week on maths and then drop it and not do any for a few months ... I gave him more and more of what he was good at. At one time he was into anatomy – we learned a lot and did a lot together.

This way of working would, of course, be impossible in most schools.

Specialist knowledge
A good grasp of their subject is essential for teachers in the classroom, but parents at home need not be specialists in any of the school subjects. A teacher who wants to give a lesson on volcanoes, for example, has to find out about the subject well before the lesson. By contrast, a parent at home may be perfectly open about the fact that they know very little about volcanoes and they may share in the child's pleasure and excitement as they find out about the subject together. Many parents comment on the unexpected bonus that home education has brought to them personally as their own knowledge has been broadened and extended as a result of working with their child.

Specialist knowledge is not needed at home because parents and children may learn together. Whether the education is structured or informal an everyday feature of it will be that a great deal of it is shared or joint learning. This is noticeable especially as children grow older and they begin to study areas that their parents know little about or have forgotten from their own schooling. If you are moving on to a new topic you can work on it and discuss it together. What you have to offer is a better understanding of how to learn, so that you act as a kind of guide. It won't matter if your child 'gets' something before you do. She'll just be pleased and it will boost her confidence.

Lesson time
It's normal for children in school to have lessons all day long and it might appear from this that school is an environment where learning takes place intensively. Surprisingly, education at home turns out to be more intensive than school as most families find that part of the day – usually mornings – spent on formal work is enough. We know that

children at school spend only two-thirds of their time on task. Even then all that we know is that they are doing something; we don't know for certain that they are learning anything. In school a lot of time is spent on non-teaching activities including registration, assembly, organizing the classroom, and dealing with all the interruptions that crop up. Also, children spend time moving around from one classroom to another. As a member of the Irish Parliament, the Dáil, pointed out in a recent debate on home education: 'Time in the classroom is not time spent learning.'

Informal learning

Another difference between school and home is the position of informal learning. The first principle of learning in school is that the teachers teach and the children learn what the teachers teach. Thus there is little room for informal learning in the school day. At home informal learning is very important and many parents discover this for themselves as they settle in to home education. Although they might have started with a full day, once they discover it's too demanding they reduce formal learning to a couple of hours a day. The children are relatively free during the rest of the day. But this doesn't mean that they don't do anything which might contribute to learning during this free time. They may read for pleasure, discuss all sorts of things with their parents, do projects which interest them, play with their friends, use the computer or help with shopping, cooking and other household tasks.

A child might describe much of this kind of activity as 'mucking around' or chatting with Mum or Dad. Obviously, at first glance these occupations seem to be just a pleasant addition to more structured or formal education. However, most parents begin to see that such activities do make a valuable contribution to learning. As time goes by they see that these casual activities are not just a supplement to structured, more formal learning, but they are of equal value, running alongside it. A few parents begin to think that what their children are learning informally, without realizing it, could even replace a lot of what they learn during structured sessions. Amanda, even though she describes herself as 'regimented', has begun to see this:

> I'm learning now to be more confident in their own interests, but I'd never leave them even though I can see them picking things up on their own. I didn't think that before. But now I can see they do it, not following the same pathway as schools but they get to the same place.

There's more on this important and little-understood type of learning in Chapter 3.

Written work

At school, children constantly produce written work as evidence of learning and achievement. At home, written work is far less important as parents usually know what stage their child has reached. In order to give his partner a break, Mark spends a morning a week working with his two children aged 8 and 6. He started off with the assumptions which most people have about teaching children:

> My first presumption was to read to them and then ask questions. After a few weeks I realized that asking questions or getting them to write answers didn't matter. It's the story that's important. We'd also got the idea you had to regurgitate stuff. But you don't need worksheets to see if it's gone in. Someone asked me if we tested them. It made me realize that testing is farcical at home.

Some parents insist on a certain amount of written work, but others often question why so much emphasis is put on writing in school. They point out that it's simply not necessary to write things down in order to learn. Also, just as you are not going to learn much from reading something in which you have little or no interest, there may be no point in writing down anything unless you have something that you want to say. In school, writing is 'evidence' that teaching and learning have taken place and it is used as a means of grading children. At home, parents know what their children can do without them having to write anything like as much as they would in school. Of course it's necessary to be able to write effectively for various purposes; that's not in question. When they are educating at home parents need to decide how much writing is actually necessary and how best to go about it.

Ticks and crosses

Marking work, grading children and testing them is seen as essential in school where one teacher is in charge of the educational progress of thirty or more children in a class, and written exercises contribute much to this process. At home there's far less need for any of these, and some would say that there is no need at all for them as mistakes or problems may be dealt with as they occur.

In school, getting back work that has been marked is fine if you've got everything right. For the majority who make mistakes, the feedback may reduce both their confidence and their desire to learn. In school the pupil has to do an exercise or homework, give it in and get it back to know whether or not the learning has been successful. By the time the homework is returned the child may well have moved on to something different anyway. This might mean that the child has to go on to the next lesson without mastering the previous one adequately. This is very unlikely to occur at home because of the one-to-one basis of home education.

Individualized teaching

Individualized teaching is rarely possible in school as the teacher has only a few minutes to spend with each child. On the other hand, almost all teaching at home is individualized. Working with a child individually means that you are always aware of the stage that the child has reached in his or her understanding of a subject. You can help the child to advance from that level and you are also able to deal with any difficulties, misunderstandings or errors there and then. Here's Conchita, aged 11:

> Sometimes I get bored with maths but I still get them all right. As soon as I get something wrong my Mum explains on the spot.

Because individualized teaching at home is an interactive process it's possible to provide instant feedback on the child's work. Home educated children tend to expect assistance as soon as they need it, and they often grumble if the help is not at hand as speedily as they would wish!

Another aspect of individualized teaching at home is that children have the opportunity to influence their learning in a way that is impossible at school. When we were in school the first thing most of us learned was to feign attention when we were not paying attention, often becoming quite expert at it! At home this doesn't work. Because it is one-to-one, parents know immediately when their children stop listening. There's just no point in going on. There is nothing as pointless or unproductive as insisting on teaching someone who is not learning.

It's not that home educated children can't adapt to the kind of teaching and learning that is found in school. They do so with little difficulty if they do start or return to school eventually. But many young people resist formal learning at home. It's important to realize that it doesn't mean that there's anything wrong. You haven't failed. It just means that it may be necessary to adapt and try another approach. One significant advantage of individualized teaching at home is that it's possible to try various ways of learning which may be radically different from the school approach. At school, of course, there is very little opportunity to do things differently.

Teaching reading

Perhaps the most significant and fundamental area of learning which differs markedly between school and home is the teaching of reading. At school reading is taught by teachers who have been trained to teach it but at home it isn't necessary for parents to have had professional training. Parents often worry about teaching this crucial skill to their children but it seems that the amount of individual attention which the child receives is the critical factor for success. Home educators use a variety of methods and approaches to reading and children at home learn at a wide range of ages. At school children are expected to have reached a certain standard by the end of Key Stage 1 but at home they may make progress at their own rate. There's more about the teaching of reading in Chapter 5.

Reading for pleasure

Related to this is the place of reading for pleasure in the school timetable. It's well known that children at school have very little time for reading during the school day. During the secondary years the demands of homework and coursework also make inroads into the time which is available for reading in the evenings. The situation is very different at home, though, where most home educated children are avid readers. Many parents report that their children read endlessly and this seems to be an important source of learning for some young people.

Working in groups

School offers opportunities for learning in groups, including activities such as drama and sport. Children at home are not prevented from taking part in group work but opportunities to join groups have to be created. There are many ways of taking part in such activities in the community for children of all ages but families have to find out what is on offer and then make their own arrangements. Chapter 8 has details of some of the group activities which young people may join from home. One advantage that home educated children have is that these activities are optional, whereas they are often compulsory at school. There is no more sure way of putting children off sport, for instance, than to force them to take part in it! Children are far more likely to take a lasting interest in group activities if they are able to choose their own level of involvement.

Social life

Finally, the social experience of school contrasts with the social life of home educated children. While children at most schools mix with many others of a similar age, children at home usually have fewer social contacts but these are with children of all ages and adults as well. As we explain in Chapter 8, there are many ways of ensuring that home educated children enjoy a full and rewarding social life even if they have never attended school.

The experience of school

Our comments above show some of the ways in which learning at home is different from learning in school. Many of the most familiar and enduring aspects of school turn out to be unnecessary or irrelevant at home. Of course certain children might miss out on some aspects of the experience of school. One of these is competition which some people might argue is a necessary preparation for life in the 'real' world. Although school constantly fosters a competitive spirit, the downside is that, by definition, only a few can succeed. When a child is educated at home and there is the opportunity to work at the child's own pace the question of competitiveness doesn't arise. Not surprisingly, competitiveness is something which virtually never features in families' descriptions of home education. Naturally, children will want to succeed when they are older and many will wish to sit public examinations. But it is not necessary for them to compete for years against their peers by way of preparation for the experience.

We mentioned at the beginning of this chapter that at first it may be difficult to imagine a form of education which is completely different from the norm of school. One way of seeing school in a rather different light, perhaps, is to imagine a country in which home education is universal. It had been universal, at least, until a number of parents got together to form something which they called a 'school', perhaps because the economic situation in the country was forcing them to go out to work. An inspector has been along to assess the education being provided in this 'school' and his report is given below:

Report on what has been called 'school education' at 'The New School', by J. Headwood, Chief Inspector of Education.

Overall conclusion
This school does not meet the requirements for effective education as outlined in the Education Act.

Reasons

1   The length of time which is required for learning at school is at least three times as long as the amount which is recommended for education at home. The justification which is given for this discrepancy is that the staff are obliged to teach large numbers of children at the same time. While this is understandable from the teachers' point of view it is not acceptable from the children's standpoint. Children simply cannot be expected both to concentrate for up to five hours a day at school and to complete a couple of hours of work at home in the evening, but the teachers insist that this is necessary for adequate progress.

2   The teachers do not interact with each child. If a child has a problem he or she has only the briefest opportunity to discuss it with the teacher, if at all. The teachers' response is that they simply cannot relate individually to each child in what they term a 'class' of 30. This is true of course but it violates the child's right to an education that is adapted to his or her needs.

3   A great deal of the children's time is devoted to writing or to completing exercises on their own. This seems to be a method of demonstrating that the children are learning. In my view this fails on two grounds. First, children's mistakes are not dealt with immediately which means that they will continue on the wrong tack if they make any errors or fail to understand the nature of the task. Second, far too much time is devoted to working alone, so that some children become bored and actually do very little. I suspect that this is also the means whereby teachers keep the children fully occupied so that they are more easily managed.

4   Much learning is supposed to occur through the teacher talking to the whole class at the same time. There is scant regard for individual children apart from the few who appear to engage with the teacher.

5   Children have to study regardless of whether or not they are learning, for example if they are tired or not interested in the 'lesson'. Of equal concern is that if they are interested and enthusiastic there is no opportunity for them to continue once the 'lesson' has ended.

6   Informal learning is recognized as an essential aspect of education. The very nature of 'school' makes this kind of learning virtually out of the question.

Recommendation: I am sympathetic with the reasons that the parents give for setting up the 'school' and employing 'teachers'. However, in order to meet with the requirements of the Education Act it would be essential to employ very many more teachers. I understand that this would be out of the question financially, so I have no option but to recommend closure.

This fictional situation is not intended as a criticism of teachers. The intention is to show that it simply does not make sense to transfer a set of expectations and procedures from the educational culture of school to the environment of home education. As we have seen, methods and approaches to learning which work well in school may be completely out of place at home.

CHAPTER 3

Informal learning

With home ed. you know a lot without learning it.
(17-year-old girl)

In the last chapter we mentioned how most parents, though not all, came to appreciate the part played by informal learning in home education. Very little is known about this kind of learning. More than this, it challenges the ideas that most people have about what education is supposed to mean for children of school age. That's why we are devoting a whole chapter to the subject. First of all we are going to look at what is known about informal learning. Then we will move on to what actually happens in informal learning.

Informal learning, by its very nature, might appear to an observer to be spontaneous, haphazard, unplanned, chaotic, incidental and generally all over the place. This makes it very difficult to describe in simple terms. We make no apologies for this. How many parents could describe how their children learned so much at home before reaching school age? This also applies if you try to describe adult informal learning. At a recent seminar on what adults learned informally through community involvement, the speaker was asked how he actually knew what was being learned. 'That's the problem,' he replied. 'You know they are learning something that's important, but you can't capture it, let alone measure it. That's what makes informal learning so frustrating and so captivating at the same time.' It is in this spirit we invite you to share the following exploration of informal learning for children of school age.

Imagine visiting two homes to find out what home education is like. In the first, the children are sitting around the table with their 'teacher–parent', working from a textbook. They ask questions from time to time as they complete a task in their exercise books. This is what anyone new to home education would probably expect to see.

Nearly everyone knows what school is like and this is similar to school.

In the second home, the first thing that will strike you is that nothing much seems to be happening. There's no sense of getting down to work, no earnest application to learning, by either the parent or the child. One child is talking with his mother about what was on television last night. Then the conversation shifts to various other topics. They continue chatting together for some time. The other child is concentrating on her Lego model, listening to the conversation with half an ear and joining in from time to time. After a while they all go shopping. When they come back the children decide they are going to dress up and play a fantasy game. Before they go off to get started you ask them if they'll show you something they've done recently. One brings you an earlier Lego model she made. The other proudly shows you a story he's written. It's quite short with lots of crossings out. Spelling and punctuation have not been corrected.

You can understand why education officials will be more at home with the first of these families!

Now let's move on a few years. The children from both homes continue to be educated in the same way until they embark on GCSE courses when they are 14. They gain equally good results. Somehow the children who learned informally made at least equal progress without careful and deliberate teaching between the ages of 5 and 14.

However structured they are in their approach, almost all parents begin to see that informal learning has an important role to play in home education. The extent to which an informal approach will be adopted will of course vary with each individual family. But you do need to think about informal learning, not least because you may find that your child resists structured teaching despite your efforts.

Many parents are naturally cautious about relying too much on informal learning. It may well prove successful for some learners, but how do I know it will suit my children? How will I know they are learning anything useful? Will they just loll about all day? What about when they get older? After learning informally, will they be able to adjust to greater formality and structure as they approach GCSE? Obviously, we cannot answer these questions definitively because there has been very little research into informal learning for children of school age. But we do know for sure that informal learning has a part to play in all children's education, including children in school who have the opportunity to learn informally when they are at home.

When children are being taught formally, it's easy to see what they are learning. When we are dealing with informal learning, it becomes necessary to pay much closer attention to what is happening, especially when, on the surface at least, a great deal seems to have little obvious purpose or direction. Let's take a closer look.

What do we know about informal learning?

Our ancestors learned everything they needed to know quite informally, talking with, watching and later working alongside those with greater expertise and knowledge. Today we still rely almost completely on informal learning for young children to learn basic skills and knowledge of the world around them. Of course we 'teach' them in one sense. But we rarely set out to do so deliberately in the school sense of planning what to teach and then teaching it. A most striking example of this is that children learn most of the complicated grammatical rules of language without any direct teaching. In fact, deliberately planned attempts to teach very young children how to talk correctly seldom work, even if a powerful reward is on offer. The following example is illustrative:

> Mother: Now drink your milk.
> Child: I not want milk.
> M: Say 'I don't want milk'.
> C: I not want milk.
> M: No, no, no. Listen carefully. Say 'I don't want milk'.
> C: I not want milk.
> M: All right. ... You don't have to drink your milk if you say it like me. If you can say 'I don't want milk' you won't have to drink it and you can have a piece of chocolate instead.
> C: [desperate to get it right] I don't not want milk.

The child obviously learned the correct construction later on, as all children do. But we can be sure that he did so informally, without realizing that he'd learned it. In other words, informal learning is very powerful.

So far, so good. It's easy to see that your children learn nearly everything informally before they start school. But, if you think about it, there's no reason why informal learning should have to stop just because children start learning formally at school. For children who start school, the opportunity for learning informally at home is suddenly and dramatically reduced. An interesting exception is for children who go to nursery school on a half-time basis when they are 3 to 4 years old. Some fascinating and very well known research compared what these children learned informally during the half day at home alongside their mothers with what they learned in the nursery class. Take into account, too, that the researchers missed out what the children were also learning in the evenings and at weekends. The authors of the research, Barbara Tizard and Martin Hughes, describe in their book *Children Learning at Home and in School* (1984) how their findings challenge the professional view that young children will learn much more at home if parents model themselves on teachers:

> a point of view that is widespread ... implies that professionals know better than parents how to educate children ... this view is mistaken. Home is by no means an inferior substitute for school. On the contrary, it provides a powerful learning environment for young children, but one that is very different from school. (p. 235)

They describe in great detail what these young children learn at home and in school. At home, children are always talking with their parents and asking questions, sometimes persistently. They share in an extensive range of everyday activities, both at home and in the local community. In brief as the authors put it:

> At home, parent and child share a common life, stretching back into the past and forward into the future. This vast body of shared experience helps the mother to understand what her child is saying, or intending to say. It also facilitates a task essential for intellectual growth – helping the child to make sense of her present experiences by relating them to past experiences, as well as to her existing framework of knowledge. (p. 250)

This was in contrast to learning in the school nursery where

> the richness, depth and variety which characterised the home conversations were sadly missing. So too was the sense of intellectual struggle, and of the real attempts to communicate being made on both sides. The questioning, puzzling child we were so taken with at home was gone ... conversations with adults were mainly restricted to answering questions rather than asking them, or taking part in minimal exchanges about the whereabouts of other children and play material. (p. 9)

This research was originally carried out to look at social class differences in the use of language by parents with their children. What the researchers found, however, was that nearly all parents provide rich learning experiences at home whatever their social class background and their level of education.

Informal learning at home is quite demanding. Children who are left to their own devices are not going to learn much. The development of infants who were brought up in orphanages in the 1940s provides a dramatic illustration of this (Goldfarb, cited in Shaffer, 1993, p. 440).

At the time the orphanages were state of the art, providing excellent levels of health care and nutrition in clean and pleasant surroundings. But the children did not develop normally. They were miles behind other children in all aspects of intellectual and emotional development. The reason? Although they were well cared for, they had very little interaction with an adult.

There is now a growing recognition of the part played by informal learning for adults as well, through conversing with friends and family, reading, the media, travel, and through their hobbies, interests and suchlike. People who train workers in industry now realize the contribution which informal learning can make. For example, when you start a new job, everything seems strange at first and there's a lot to learn. A year later and you've acquired a great deal of 'know-how' without realizing it. Some research has shown that short courses such as induction or computer courses may not be as effective as just doing the job and getting help as and when you need it from your more experienced colleagues. Even advanced professional knowledge, in law and medicine for example, is often acquired informally (Gear *et al*, 1994).

Returning to the question of children's learning, we can say that by the time they reach school age they have already acquired a massive amount of knowledge. Almost all of this knowledge has been gained informally. In addition to having an excellent grasp of spoken language and a fast growing vocabulary they will probably be well on the way to reading, having been playing with and recognizing letter shapes, their own names and other familiar words, following stories which their parents read to them, as well as recognizing shop signs, especially advertisements for fast food and ice cream! They will have at least a basic grasp of essential maths skills: counting, adding and subtracting, knowledge of shapes and so on. We don't mean maths which has been deliberately taught as it is in school. We mean real world maths which is part and parcel of everyday activity. It may be a simple activity, centred around getting some sweets, for instance. It's such an ordinary part of everyday life at home that neither parent nor child will be aware of learning any maths. Take the following typical ways of learning about important basic concepts:

Addition (+): You've got three Smarties. Here are two more. How many have you got now?
More than (>) and less than (<) and equal (=): Who's got more Smarties? Have I got less than you? Is that fair now?
Subtraction (−): Drat, I said you could only have three Smarties but I've tipped out some more. How many did I tip out? Take

your three away and let's see. How many left? I think you ought to
have the others anyway, don't you?

All the time, too, they will be expanding their general knowledge by
listening, asking interminable questions, getting involved in household
activities and shopping, going on visits and so on.

So, if your child is learning happily at home as school age approaches, why not just continue in the same vein? This is how a
number of home educators start, trying it out for a year or so to see
how it goes. Most children now start half-time nursery school at 3 and
full-time education at 4. Statutory schooling does not start until they
are 5. So you can even 'educate' your child at home for two years
without actually being a 'home educator'. If you need reassurance you
can compare them with DfES Early Learning Goals and Baseline Assessment standards which are readily available. Later on you can
compare with Key Stage levels if you wish. There is very little risk
involved unless not starting school early might mean losing a place for
your child at your preferred school.

What do 'informal' parents and children actually do?
If you follow a curriculum package or work from texts, at least you
know that your children are learning more or less what they would be
taught if they were in school. This does not mean that parents who rely
on informal learning go ahead in a void. Obviously, they have the
intention of ensuring that their children will get the knowledge and
skills they are going to need later on, especially literacy, numeracy and
a good general knowledge. Parents then take opportunities to develop
these as they arise during the course of everyday living, suggesting
activities which might interest their children, or responding to what
catches their children's attention. We don't want to suggest that
parents are constantly on the lookout for 'learning' opportunities. That
would kill informal learning which by its nature is spontaneous.

Let's start with Alison talking about her two daughters aged 9 and 7
who have never been in school:

> There's no pattern or calendar or timetable. We are still very
> haphazard – something will happen and we'll follow it from there.
> For example, I'm interested in geology. We were digging yesterday
> and found some ochre type stuff that dissolves in water. I'd like to
> find out what it is. We get books out of the library, ask people and
> eventually find out what kind of rock it is.
>   We talk a lot.

Eilean describes her informal approach for her two boys of 9 and 7:

We are completely lax. We [parents] are always doing our own thing around the house which creates an atmosphere of doing things. Geoff gets the children involved in doing models. They've made a sundial which led to working out latitude.

David wakes up first but is very quiet. He does sums on his hands before he gets up. While I was there this morning he threw out the answer to 2 × 1.55 and another similar one – these had arisen in the course of shopping or some such activity. Sometimes they both come into bed with me and we talk. This morning Kes told me that the sun goes red ten minutes before we see it. Breakfast is about 9.30ish. After watching some TV, mostly school programmes, they go out to play – poke around in the pond, climb a tree, make magic potions out of petals, etc. During the day we might go to the library – when we get there they just sit down and read and read and read. Yesterday afternoon we all went to the garden centre to measure the pipes in a garden wind chime for one we wanted to make. This led to talking about sound frequencies related to the length of the pipes.

Eilean may describe her approach as 'completely lax'. By this she doesn't mean lazy or sloppy. She finds informal learning quite exhausting. As she says: 'They even hate us being on the phone because this means we are not available for them.'

Eilean has two concerns. The first is that the boys

abandon a lot of activities once their curiosity has been satisfied. For example, it's what happened with making bread and biscuits, stamp and coin collection. It's the same for looking after the hen in the garden, though they still like collecting the eggs.

She also thinks the boys now need something in addition to what they can offer. As she puts it: 'Generally, I think they need more complexity, more layers.' This may be because parents who educate their children informally give much more of themselves than they would if they were following a text or other programme. After a time you might feel the children need input from other people.

By way of international comparison, there are even informal home educators in Japan although home education is quite rare. In fact, home education is not recognized as an acceptable alternative to school. Instead, children are described as 'school refusers'. A Japanese mother, Tomoko, talks about her 9-year-old son Minori's very informal home education:

Minori gets up between 8.00 and 9.00 a.m. He reads books and magazines. Every two weeks he borrows fifteen books from the library. This takes him to lunch. After lunch, he uses the computer and plays games on it, makes things, goes into the garden, goes to the park to play ball, or out on the front pavement with chalk to play games. Then my daughter comes home from school and they play. Then dinner and TV or reading or he plays games with her. When my husband comes home they play together with the computer and internet sometimes. He goes to bed between 12.00 and 1.00 a.m. After he goes to bed he reads books until he goes to sleep.

Minori asks lots of questions, like he did before he went to school. He stopped asking questions when he went to school. After he'd been home for three months he started asking questions again. He asks many, many questions, like 'Why is the sky blue?' I'm a bit tired with all the questions but it's nice.

Incidentally, because he is a school refuser, he will not be able to enter university in Japan. To overcome this, his parents eventually enrolled him in an English speaking school so that he could apply to universities outside the country.

Talking, talking, talking

If there's one thing about informal education which stands out above all others, it's conversation. On the face of it much of this is social, everyday talk which normally goes unnoticed. But this kind of talk contains many learning opportunities, especially as the conversation is between a child and an adult whose knowledge of the world and how to find out things is obviously much greater. Even home educators whose approach is quite formal commonly remark on the importance of the talking that they do with their children. The following gives a sense of the variety of what different parents say about talking with their children and its contribution to learning:

> There's a lot of interaction and learning while they're doing things, including about how we relate as a family, principles for life.

> When watching [television] programmes (documentary, musical, science) it's the talking that goes with them. The real learning goes with this, talking and dialogue while watching together, and with reading.

> We have a lot of discussions. He absorbs more information in a discussion than at any other time, e.g. why do we have bonfire night – he remembered the information and it led on to a discussion of Parliament.

Conversation is important, yes, very, because as a family we talk quite a lot to each other. They learn to express themselves and they find out a lot of things through conversation. You can bounce things back at them and help build their vocabulary.

An important part of informal conversational learning is that children's questions get answered immediately. As Tomoko found, her son's constant questioning stopped when he started school but resumed after he began to learn at home at 8 years of age. We often smile at young children's persistent questioning. This should not obscure the fact that the best learning is likely to occur when you get immediate answers to questions that you want to ask. This kind of questioning is neatly captured by the term 'intellectual search', coined by Barbara Tizard and Martin Hughes in their book from which we quoted above. They go on to ponder the role of conversational learning:

> We have no reason to suppose that the process of education through one-to-one dialogue ... needs to take place all day and every day. It may be that one episode of real concentration each day, or one question seriously answered, is as valuable as hours of less focused attention ... we do not believe that parents must always answer their children's questions and constantly engage in long conversations with them. We suspect, however, that children whose parents tend to answer their questions more fully, who are usually alert to detect and clear up misunderstandings, and who sometimes have time for leisurely, thoughtful conversations will make more rapid intellectual progress. (Tizard and Hughes, 1984, p. 260)

Informal conversation obviously doesn't follow any linear or logical sequence. What leads from one topic to another is difficult to fathom, but that's how most natural conversation goes. The point is that it is natural. Just as in adult social conversation, if a topic comes up about which one person knows more than the other, it is likely that one will learn from the other. It is a natural part of conversation for one person to explain something to someone else. This is not 'teaching' in the usual sense. It's simply ensuring the normal flow of talk, offering knowledge and responding to questions. Of course not everything is taken in. A lot will be forgotten. But that's not important. What is important is that some things will be remembered, to be picked up at another time perhaps. Even more striking is that the learning is not 'work' as it is in school. It is learning without knowing you are learning.

Opportunities for this kind of learning also arise in families who rely mainly on structure, even during the course of structured teaching itself. If something occurs to your child or to you which is unrelated to the task in hand it is natural to deal with it. It might be as simple as 'What's for lunch?', in which case the flow of the lesson is hardly interrupted. Or it might be a more searching question or observation in which case it would be a lost opportunity to let it go. It might even mean postponing the lesson for another time. The big advantage is that your child will be focusing on something which is of interest and therefore it is more likely to be learned.

How do you capture informal learning? It's not easy to see progress on a day-to-day or even on a month-to-month basis. A lot of learning seems to occur in unrelated bits and pieces. This would rightly be considered haphazard and sloppy in school, even unprofessional. Yet at home, somehow or other 'all these bits and pieces eventually come together like pieces in a jigsaw puzzle', as one parent put it. Informal learning has its own kind of pattern, a pattern that suits the child as understanding is gradually acquired. It simply does not conform to the way most of us expect to see progress. The logic behind the pattern is established by the child. It's a kind of individual fuzzy logic, not linear logic of the kind associated with structured learning.

Informal learning can lead to systematic and advanced study

Imagine you are talking with your child in the car and you get stuck in a traffic jam. You throw up your arms in exasperation: 'God! If this jam doesn't clear we're going to be late, again!' Your child asks: 'Why does "jam" mean two things?' You answer that a lot of words have two meanings and both of you think up examples for a few minutes and then go quiet again or start talking about something else. You could call this a morsel of informal learning. Or your child might have asked: 'Why are there traffic jams?' or 'Were there traffic jams before cars?' or you might have gone on to discuss road rage. You could go on and on thinking of the different directions a conversation could take following your initial outburst. Wherever the conversation led there would be plenty of opportunity to extend informal or incidental learning, not that you'd normally describe it as such. The chances are that by the time you get to the end of your journey you'll have both forgotten the conversation because it was just 'chatting in the car'. The only way that you would know if anything had registered would be if it came up at another time.

Once in a while a chance remark might lead to an interesting conversation or an in-depth study. The car conversation above could lead to a study of the reasons why people travel or a survey to discover the proportion that travel by car, commercial vehicle, bus and bike. It could lead to an investigation into the whole history of transport. Or you might find yourselves researching road rage, anger and aggression. In other words, this short, interesting conversation might end up as a much longer discussion; you might continue by reading up about the subject or you might begin a relatively formal project or course of study which lasts for weeks or longer. Of course, the child would not be concerned with the learning implications of the initial conversation, but would simply be finding out about something of interest. It is still informal in that no one has told the child to do it, nothing was planned beforehand and there is no predetermined sequence of learning. The child is also at liberty to drop it at any time. As a parent, your role will be to encourage, help, guide and share in the learning. Even quite young children can apply themselves to an activity when they become enthusiastic about it, as the parents of these two children relate:

> Jackie (aged 7) will concentrate for long periods if she wants to master something. Once she has made something, for example a paper lantern, she will 'go into production' so that it becomes second nature to her.

> Phases of interest sometimes last over a very long period. Charlie (aged 7) played computer games for a long time, from 6.00 to 8.00 every morning until she suddenly lost interest.

When they become enthusiastic about a subject, older children at home have plenty of opportunity to become genuine (not child) experts. Apart from the popular interests of computing, dinosaurs, volcanoes and horses, they can become enthused by a very wide range of topics. Here are just a few examples we know of which started off informally: organic egg production; Mary, Queen of Scots; competitive dog breeding; politics, including the Russian Revolution and Fascism; filigree; chemistry, motor mechanics and community action.

We are not claiming that only home educated children can develop interests in depth which are sparked off informally, but we would point out that they have more time and opportunity to do so. This example concerns someone known to us who was in school. His moribund interest in the piano was suddenly revitalized informally and this led to a quantum leap in learning. When he was 11, he had been learning the piano for three years formally and was still struggling laboriously towards a Grade 1 level. One of his teachers told his parents that he simply wasn't musical. He did everything he could to avoid practising, no doubt looking forward to the day when his parents would accept he wasn't getting anywhere and give up.

Then one day he happened to hear a piece of music few could fail to be captured by: Beethoven's Moonlight Sonata. He listened to it from time to time. For a while he just listened as he would to any other background music that he liked. All of a sudden he decided he had to play it, so his parents got hold of an easier version of the first movement, at about Grade 4 level. He spent hours poring over it until he had mastered it, in about three weeks – it takes longer if you're in school because you haven't got as much time.

A musical friend who visited spent an hour helping him with expression. Then he performed the piece in school. The family moved soon after this and he went to a new piano teacher. By now he had also taught himself a similar version of the Pathétique Sonata. His new teacher asked him to play something so she could gauge his ability. When he did, she astounded him and his family by telling him he was at a Grade 5 level. Although he was pleased, he didn't further his ability in classical music to any great extent. But he now knew he had the confidence to master what interested him – popular music and, later, jazz. He went on to become a professional jazz musician.

What about older children?

It's entirely reasonable to expect that you can continue to educate your child informally after the age of 5. In many countries, children do not start school until they are 6 or 7. It's also reasonable to expect children to go on learning through the primary years without formal lessons on the basis that much of what they learn in school is what parents already know or use on a day-to-day basis. But how far can you go? Children are not going to 'pick up' French or algebra through the course of everyday living.

Let's imagine what might happen. Your child is 10 or 11 and it is apparent to you that this young learner has a wide general knowledge and good literacy and numeracy skills. Our advice here is utterly simple. You go on as long as you and your child are happy with progress. You might gradually introduce more formal learning, in maths and a language, for example. Or you might not. Or you might decide that school is the best option.

What if you decide to continue informally? We don't have much to go on because we don't know of many children who have been informally educated well into the secondary years. But we do think it is likely that as long as children are learning, whatever they are learning, they will have few problems in dealing with a two-year GCSE course from the age of 14 if they have been informally educated. A number of young people who have been informally educated up to this age have gone on to be highly successful in public examinations. Just think of maths. There are even children who have not studied maths formally until they embarked on GCSE and then they have been successful. This is in comparison with 10 years of maths had they been in school, at least 2500 hours of deliberate and structured teaching of the subject.

Here, very briefly, are two examples of children who were educated informally until they were 16. The first, Paul, when he reached the age of 12, took charge of his own education and pursued his own interests, seeking guidance only when he needed it. His mother explains:

> Paul is now just 16 and has had a final inspection – the inspector spent 1¼ hours talking with him and was very pleased. He spends most of his time playing and composing music though he cannot read music. Then there's computing, art and writing – though he never shows any of this to us. We do not know what he will do now but are leaving it up to him to decide. He is possibly thinking about architecture.

The second is Rowena, an Australian girl who was educated almost entirely informally until she went to the last year of school, prior to going to university. This is how her mother looked back on her approach when Rowena was 16:

> It was very informal with Rowena up to Grade 10 – there was very little structure. When I think back, things did happen, but I didn't think of planning them ... (I've got to plan now because I have four younger children between 5 and 11). ... Then we panicked in Grade 10. People tell you about what you need to do to get jobs. I got worried, but we didn't do much more. We'd work really hard for a few days, then it would be informal again. We couldn't keep up the formal work. We still can't ... I've been told I should keep records – including what they do. But I've not kept records; it's the doing that matters.

Even when Rowena was formally studying prescribed material during her last six months at home, prior to going to school, they both found they could only keep it up for a couple of weeks at a time. So how did she get on? Academically, she did very well in the year she spent at school and went on to university.

The world-famous Summerhill school provides a rather different example of informal learning. Summerhill is one of the few schools where older children have the opportunity to learn informally. The philosophy of the school is that children should control their own lives. Whether or not you agree with this philosophy is not at issue. The point here is that this is probably as near as a school can get to informal learning. At the primary level, the very good pupil : teacher ratio of about eight : one means that informal learning is quite feasible.

Strangely, very few pupils miss lessons at this level. Going to the classroom is just what they all do every day. Then, typically, as lessons become more formal at the early secondary level, many children tend not to go, for a couple of years even. What is startling is that even those who miss maths for as much as two years prior to GCSE are able to catch up in just a few weeks. In fact, Summerhill fares quite favourably in comparison with national GCSE results.

Recently, Summerhill was inspected by the Office for Standards in Education (OFSTED).

Briefly, the report was quite damning. The main criticism was that children who missed lessons could not be learning anything. The Department for Education and Employment (DfEE) issued an official 'Notice of Complaint' against the school. If lessons were not made compulsory then the school would lose its registration and it would have to be closed down. The school appealed against the Complaint. The hearing took place at the Royal Courts of Justice in March 2000. It was scheduled to last two weeks but the DfEE withdrew on the third day, basically agreeing to allow the school to continue, its philosophy unchanged, as it has been for 80 years. Part of the successful Appeal was to show that children can learn a great deal informally, especially when there are older children and adults to mix with for much of the day. The DfEE accepted this and actually stated that an expert witness report which was submitted by Alan, based largely on informal learning of children educated at home, should be taken into account in any future inspections. Based on a discussion with the children, his report also detailed 116 out-of-lesson activities which could contribute to learning in various ways. Here is a selection:

Art, astronomy, bird watching, board games, collecting things, computing, cooking, creative writing, doing e-mail, exploring the countryside, visiting places of interest, going on trips – to poetry evenings, theatre etc., handiwork, knitting, sewing, embroidery, playing cards, reading, spending time with grown-ups – talking about this and that, talking about life problems, woodwork, writing letters.

Sue's experience of informal learning
In what follows we try to give you a more detailed insight into one child's experience of informal learning.

Sue's daughter Alice, now aged 13, has never been in school. From the beginning, Sue found herself relying almost totally on informal learning. She became so fascinated by it that she kept a very detailed journal of her child's informal education, including the most fleeting morsels of learning, over a period of five years. It is a unique and fascinating account of day-by-day, even minute-by-minute, informal learning, mainly through things that crop up in the course of everyday life.

Sue was never ideologically committed to informal learning, and when Alice reached the age of 11 she devised a much more structured programme which she has since been following. She tried to introduce structure a few times while Alice was still young, but it never seemed to work out and was invariably abandoned. In common with many home educators who do rely on informal learning, Sue had doubts:

> Last night I was feeling that Alice's home ed. is leading nowhere ... I feel like we just seem to have a whole heap of false starts which we fail to follow up, a bag of bits and pieces which aren't forming anything concrete.

However, she did notice that though much learning appeared inconsequential and 'leading nowhere' as she put it, when she looked back, she could see patterns of learning, even in maths. It is as if Alice is putting her own 'structure' on what she is learning, working things out for herself and in her own way. What might seem to an observer to be 'all over the place learning' is nothing of the kind for Alice. Her progress during the primary years strongly supports the view that the kind of learning that suits children in the first few years of life can be extended and modified through the primary years at the very least.

In his book *Educating Children at Home* Alan Thomas (2000) describes in detail how Sue's daughter, Alice, progressed in maths between the ages of 7 and 9½ without any structured teaching whatsoever. The reason for focusing on maths is that this is the subject that most people would think hardest to learn informally. If maths can be learnt informally, anything can.

The first thing you'd notice if you looked into the journal is just how chaotic informal learning is. Things are learned and forgotten. Sometimes Alice knows things way beyond her and at other times she seems to regress. Even though her mother assiduously notes down everything she can, Alice sometimes shows she has learned something quite substantial without her mother having any idea how she acquired it. For example, Sue noted in the journal when Alice first showed an interest in telling the time. Then, a year or so later Alice has somehow learned to tell the time accurately. But the journal contains next to nothing in between about how she did it.

Maths

Let's look in more detail at Alice learning maths. The first excerpt is taken from Alan's book when Alice was just 7. The second excerpt is more recent, when Alice had just turned 10. It's real life maths.

> In the first example, Alice is aged 7 and is going to the shops and back.
> [In the car]
> Alice: Those numbers on that bus add up to 10.
> Sue: Yes, that's right. And what is the number they make standing side by side?
> A: One hundred and forty-five.
> M: Yes, that's the number of the bus. Bus number one hundred and forty-five .... .
>
> [Walking past a shop]
> A: What's one point zero zero?
> M: It's one dollar.
>
> A: Are you buying that ruler for me?
> M: Yes. I know you already have a ruler, but this one has the cms marked out very clearly. It'll help you learn the cms.
> (M: Alice comes over to have a closer look. She counts the cms from 0 to 30).
>
> [On the way home in the car].
> A: It's six years until I'm 13.
> M: Well done, to work that out.
> A: I did it with add ups in my head. I like to do lots of add ups and take aways in my head. (Thomas, 2000, pp. 86-7)

In this example, Sue involved Alice in a family project, to make a picket fence to keep the dogs out of the vegetable garden. Afterwards, Sue wrote down in great detail how they proceeded together. Then she summarized the maths that had cropped up during the activity:

> measuring in cms
> the terms opposite and parallel
> addition into 100s
> multiplication with known tables
> division
> decimals
> money calculations

This was a real life task. After working out how close the pickets would have to be to prevent the dogs getting through, they then calculated how many would be needed in total. They went to the hardware store, only to find they could not afford so many. They would have to find another way of enclosing the vegetable garden.

Sustained learning – Italian

Sue did not formally decide to teach Alice Italian. It started from Sue's own interest in the language and she invited Alice to learn with her, as a 'fun thing' from when Alice was 2 years old. From the beginning, Alice joined in the learning only as long as she wanted to. In this sense it was informal. It was not pursued methodically. They dropped and picked it up again and again, especially when they reached a plateau or lost interest. But it was always there in the background. That's how it has proceeded for at least ten years: drop it, for months or longer and pick it up again. As Sue once said: 'On the subject of Italian, I love it but ... I often find my own incentive for learning it hanging by a thread. Alice is only lukewarm too.' Recently the interest was re-awakened and they both enrolled in an adult education class. So they continue ... .

Alice's progress

As we've said, Sue was never sure about informal learning. She kept an eye on Alice's progress by checking it against what she would have been doing had she been in school. But there's nothing like independent verification.

When Alice was 11 she entered the University of New South Wales Maths and English competitions which are held annually. This is intended for schools to enter pupils they think will do at least reasonably well. In each test she achieved a 'Credit' which is well above average performance in this selected group. Sue was delighted:

> How much deliberate formal maths or English has Alice ever done? Little compared with the hours spent on them in schools. It really says something when one knows that the private schools all make a big thing of these tests. I'm sorry I'm crowing so dreadfully, but it's exciting, I just feel thrilled to bits. And, just after the test, she had said to me that she thought she went badly because 'there wasn't enough time to do it properly'.

This progress is further confirmed by independent reports by the Australian home education monitor who is a teacher with a full understanding of the different approaches to home education. Here is a report made when Alice was 12. The monitor notes that Alice's education is now becoming more structured:

> Alice's home education continues to address her all round development through a largely holistic, natural approach to life and learning. Some structure has been introduced this year in light of Alice's reaching 'secondary level' age and stage of development ... The introduction of some structure to the learning approach means that Alice now works from a few core text books, usually in a time set aside each morning for concentrated work.

The report then goes into some detail regarding literacy, numeracy and other aspects. With regard to numeracy, the monitor highlights the transition from informal to structured learning, clearly accepting that Alice is expected to learn some secondary maths informally as well:

> Alice's learning in maths has been predominantly through everyday numeracy skill requirements. A secondary-level text has been purchased with a view to addressing areas not covered through 'real maths' ... and the emphasis on everyday maths will continue.

Incidentally, the monitor, in common with anyone trying to get a handle on informal learning, found it difficult to summarize Alice's educational experience:

> [I] would like to comment that choosing aspects of Alice's home education to mention in this report, from those that had to be excluded from the veritable plethora of activities and resources was by no means an easy task!

A final word ... There has been very little research into informal learning for children of school age. It is also difficult to define and pin down. What we do know is that a heavy reliance on informal learning can be successful. Whether this would be so for all children we do not know. In this chapter we have simply tried to give you some insights into this subject. How far you adopt an informal approach is obviously up to you. But you can be sure that informal learning will have at least some part to play in home education however structured it is.

CHAPTER 4

Starting out

Once you have decided to go ahead with education at home, there are a number of practicalities to consider. What effect will home education have on your family life, and what impact will it have on your home and on your career? Whether your child's learning at home starts from the beginning or after being at school for some years, you will find that it makes a big difference to everything. In this chapter we'll consider these questions before moving on to look at some educational matters.

Attitudes of family and friends

Family and friends may not always approve of your decision to educate your child at home. While some people may be supportive, be prepared for a certain amount of criticism as people sometimes feel threatened by your decision. Fay comments:

> My sister-in-law was very shocked when she heard that the children weren't going to attend school. It was over a year before she would talk about it at all. I didn't realize at the time that she had taken our decision as a personal criticism as she had children in the school system. It was tough at first as I didn't feel very confident myself, and it would have been easy to allow myself to be undermined by the opposition which I encountered. I had to make an extra special effort not to be put off by anyone and I had to keep reminding myself that no one else knew our children as well as we did.

It's important to be positive even when people are critical. Margaret says:

> Don't let other people put you off! Believe in yourself and, above all, believe in your child and enjoy your learning together. You don't have to be a teacher to do it, especially as there is so much information which is freely available these days. Schools haven't

been around for very long when you think about it. They were probably essential in the days when there were masses of parents who only had a very elementary education, so they weren't that well equipped to do it themselves. But now we live in a very different world. When you announce your decision you may find that people are hostile, but they soon get used to the idea that your children are not going to school. And it's great when they begin to admit that they are impressed, although they thought you were mad at first!

Sometimes your path might be a lonely one at the beginning. Yolande remembers:

When I took Holly out of school I must admit that I felt isolated as I was cut off from my 'peer group'. We live in a small village and we soon found that we were not welcome around the other families once word got around that we were educating at home. I suppose the other mothers thought that we might lead their children astray! We didn't choose home education ... circumstances in school forced it on us so we just had to make the best of it. It was a great help to both of us to meet up with other home educators although we had to travel quite a distance to do so. We joined a national home education organization and it was very reassuring to belong to something. We definitely felt stronger when we knew that we were not alone.

Parents often comment on the invaluable support which they received from other home educators after they joined one of the national groups. In the early stages it's particularly helpful to hear of the experiences of other families who are well established in home education.

Around the house

There will be an impact upon life around the house. Home education tends to give rise to large amounts of creative activity, equipment, books and materials which have to be accommodated somewhere. Add the presence of a child or children and the house usually becomes less tidy and more housework is generated. Take away the time which you will want to give to your children's education, and you may wonder if your home will ever recover!

Where will your home education take place? Two families who have home educated from the beginning give their views. Janet recalls the way that life changed for her family:

We didn't really think much about the effect that education at home would have on our lifestyle. At the time we were still deep in the muddle of the pre-school years and we just carried on without any special strategy for home education. When my eldest child reached school age I had a 3-year-old and I was expecting a baby as well, and we just had vague thoughts that we would probably need some more bookshelves soon.

Well, as time went by the house seemed to shrink! We began to run out of walls for displaying paintings and alphabet friezes and collages made with lentils and tissue paper, and every windowsill and shelf became home to models of Stevenson's *Rocket*, *Mallard* and an endless variety of seafaring vessels made from cereal boxes. Under our bed became a treasure trove of Pringles containers, back numbers of *National Geographic* and useful electrical bits from discarded toys and old computers. It was so crammed under there that even the spiders gave up in the end!

The kitchen was a haven for carrot tops in saucers sprouting enormous foliage, improbable objects made from playdough and test-tube racks with ominous and long-forgotten mixtures lurking within the glassware. Home education got into every corner of the house and garden, especially when friends came to join us and we made up plays or did science experiments or origami. Learning at home was so much a part of life that it would have been impossible to confine it to one room. It just happened everywhere that we were.

Helen and Tony decided on a different approach. Helen says:

When we decided on home education we wanted to make it really special for the children. We turned the spare room into a schoolroom so that we could have everything together. Rebecca is 9 now and she loves to be able to work in there in peace with Sarah, who is two years younger. The twins are only 4 and the older ones need a place where they can be undisturbed. We have a big table in the middle of the room and lots of shelves round the sides. They have stacking boxes for art materials and a tea chest for all the wonderful craft bits that we get from a scrap store. The Lego models and nature collections stay in the schoolroom too so that the little ones don't spoil them. At the moment Sarah and Rebecca are making a puppet theatre out of a big cardboard box in there and we're not allowed to see it until it's ready! They are responsible for keeping it tidy themselves, but if they're in the middle of a messy project I help them to get straight again when they're finally finished.

As you will have extra demands on your time it makes sense to encourage the children to take some responsibility for washing up, shopping, preparing meals, sharing the care of younger siblings, vacuum cleaning, keeping things tidy and other basic jobs around the home. A lot depends upon the age of the children, of course, but even small ones are able to be useful and many are keen on 'helping'. It is a matter for individual parents to decide on whether they will insist on it if their children are reluctant to do their share, but if they are willing to help it may ease the burden on the parent and give useful experience to the child.

Parents and home education

Many people ask whether or not home education is compatible with a career for the parent who stays at home. We have found that parents often have to make the difficult choice between taking responsibility for their children's education and following their own career, but some people manage to achieve a working compromise. If you are fortunate enough to be working from home already, you may be able to continue by organizing your commitments to fit in with the children's learning. Home education doesn't have to take up the whole day and you may be able to arrange for the children to spend some of their time with relatives or friends.

Although it's likely that educating children at home will involve some sacrifices, there are sure to be compensations as well. Meeting other families and making friends with them may more than make up for being at home and out of the social environment of the workplace. Most families are glad to meet others in order to extend their children's social life and good friendships may be made between parents as well as between children.

You will certainly learn a great deal as you support and encourage your children's learning, and parents sometimes find that they become interested in taking up further study themselves. This may be anything from recreational study of a foreign language to research leading to a higher degree.

Educational matters

Before we look at some of the different ways in which children learn and the approaches to home education which families adopt, we'll say something about the national curriculum (the 5–14 guidelines in Scotland) as it's synonymous with education in many people's minds. The national curriculum is compulsory only in maintained schools, but does it have implications for home educators?

Although a small number of home educators follow the national curriculum and some families use it as a rough guide, most families pay little attention to it. The national curriculum was intended to ensure equality of opportunity in education, but its critics say that it is overloaded and too academic. Many of its young 'beneficiaries' are disaffected and resentful about being forced to study subjects which are of no interest to them, and some of these are turning to home education to find the freedom of choice which they cannot have at school.

We know of a significant number of school pupils for whom the national curriculum is not an entitlement but a hindrance. There is the case of Charlotte, for example, who is a 13 year-old Romany Traveller girl. Charlotte went to a primary school but by the beginning of her secondary education she was lost. She spent two terms at secondary school where she was miserable, frightened and bullied by staff and pupils alike. During this time she was expected to study the full national curriculum, including German and science. She could not read well enough to understand her books and worksheets in any subject and she was in despair by the time her parents took her out of the school.

Charlotte has been learning at home for the past two years. She is happy absorbing her culture and learning many practical things from her parents, and she spends a morning with her tutor once a week. Work is set for the week at home. The weekly sessions concentrate on literacy and numeracy and some general knowledge is also introduced through some of the texts used and through conversation. The other important priority is for Charlotte to be competent in everyday maths. The national curriculum had absolutely no relevance for her; it was a millstone round her neck which prevented her from making progress. Unfortunately, Charlotte's experience is not unique. Young people from all cultures and backgrounds may have similar difficulties particularly if they are not fluent in reading and writing by the time they reach secondary age.

Another difficulty with the national curriculum is the preoccupation with the concept of a balanced educational experience. If they are not allowed to specialize, where will the writers and the inventors and the musicians and the artists of the future come from? In his recent biography of Yehudi Menuhin, who was educated at home, Humphrey Burton (2000) describes the boy's early years which were packed with practice, concerts, tours and lessons with leading violinists in the USA and Europe. Would the LEA's inspector have objected to the lack of breadth and balance? What would the world have lost if the Menuhins had been served with a school attendance order as a result?

Every home educating family has to make their own decisions about the nature of their learning at home, but our investigations show that

the national curriculum is usually quickly set aside once families become confident and established in home education.

Ways of learning

It is known that people learn in many different ways. Children's individual learning styles are determined by many factors, including their
personality and temperament. The one-to-one nature of home education makes it possible for parents to discover and use the ways of
learning which are most natural and rewarding to each child. You can
find out how your child learns best simply by observation and by asking
yourself questions like the following:

- Does your child enjoy making things?
- Does your child enjoy learning with real things in real situations?

If the answer to these questions is yes, your child will benefit from
hands-on activities: approach as much of your home education as
possible through practical situations.

- Is the process of making important to your child?

Your child may enjoy longer projects. Don't insist upon tasks being
finished.

- Or is the end product more important than the process?

Be prepared to help with the less interesting bits, and prepare fiddly
bits beforehand. Offer short, focused, practical tasks.

- Does your child enjoy reasoning and working things out?
- Does your child like solving problems?

Try to make as much use as possible of puzzles, wordsearches, quizzes,
etc.; focus on activities which require logical thinking; try technology
challenges and related activities.

- Does your child tend to jump intuitively to conclusions or does
  he or she follow a logical process to get there?

Don't worry if you can't always follow your child's reasoning in maths
and problem-solving, and don't worry your child about it! Many
mathematicians say that any method which works is valid as long as
they get the right answers.

- Does your child enjoy telling stories?
- Is information remembered better if it is given verbally?
- Does your child learn well through discussion?
- Does your child like to share ideas with others?

Try to present as many activities as possible verbally. Listen to your child, read and talk to your child, explore topics together. Use a tape recorder. Give your child opportunities to share new discoveries with you so that you can write them down.

- Does your child like to be organized, with a predictable routine and structure?

Keep to a routine if possible, and experiment until you find the level of structure which suits your child – and you. Some compromise may be necessary! Show your child how to keep books and materials organized and make sure there is storage space and room to keep the work tidy.

- Does your child like change and variety?
- Does your child dislike being organized, preferring surprises and spontaneity?

Keep your child interested by offering varied activities, outings and so on which you have planned or prepared in advance; informal learning may particularly suitable.

- Is your child imaginative?
- Is your child able to empathize with someone else's situation?

Your child may enjoy drama, role-play, fiction, poetry; subjects such as history, geography and English may come alive if you approach them through the imagination – putting your child in the situation of someone in another time or place.

- Does your child need lots of approval?
- Does your child work best alone or with others?

Try to arrange for your child to do some learning with other children; consider clubs, courses and group activities in your area.

- What kind of activities engage your child for the longest amount of time?
- What things does your child tire of quickly?

You may notice that your child's preferred learning styles change as you go along, so it's important to be adaptable.

Approaches to home education

As we explained in Chapter 1, education law throughout the UK gives parents the right to determine the nature of their children's education. Home educating parents adopt a great variety of methods and approaches as a result. These vary from the completely structured to the totally informal, with most families' arrangements coming somewhere in the middle. In order to help you to find your own way forward, we have divided these approaches very broadly into three groups: the structured, the semi-formal and the informal educators. Our observations suggest that the semi-formal group is by far the largest as most families have elements of both informality and structure in their home education arrangements. We make no judgements about the philosophical and moral issues which lie behind any of these positions and we stress that each family must come to their own conclusions about which approach will suit them best.

A structured approach

Lesley and Vincent chose a structured home education for their children, the eldest of whom is 12:

> We have four children, and our eldest daughter went to a small school for nearly two years at the beginning until my husband's job took us abroad for a year. The company paid for a distance learning course for her while we were in the Middle East, and she enjoyed doing the workbooks that they sent each month. When we came back to the UK we decided to try home education although we would have to pay for the materials ourselves.
>
> We decided that we wanted the children to follow a purchased curriculum and we found some courses that we liked that are produced in the United States. By the time they were all enrolled on the courses it was becoming quite expensive, but I found that I could cover the cost by taking on a few pupils as I was a piano teacher before the children were born. Textbooks are supplied where they are needed but most of the material is contained in big workbooks. There is one for each of the main school subjects so apart from music, art, reading and physical activities all our work is planned for us. Each of the children has a target of a certain number of pages per day to work through and we start after breakfast when rooms have been tidied and pets have been fed. We have a big dining room and everyone sits round the table with their books. I spend some time with each child in turn while the others are getting on with their work. Most afternoons we play in the garden, have friends round or go out to meetings with other home educators.

Structured approaches to home education include the more formal methods of working to a timetable which may or may not be based on the national curriculum, following a purchased curriculum or correspondence course and employing tutors. Some parents are committed to providing what they consider to be a good solid education along traditional lines. Some like to start the process when their children are 5, and others believe that a structured education is appropriate as the children grow older. Many families find that carefully structured provision is helpful for older learners who are preparing for GCSE as good organization is essential to avoid stress towards the end of the course.

Starting out on a formal path will require some planning and probably a timetable and a careful choice of material. You may be able to obtain sample material from suppliers of curricula so that you can try it out first. You may find that as you gain confidence and settle in to home education, what seemed essential in those first anxious weeks suddenly becomes less important.

Parents who want a structured approach often consider using a ready-made curriculum. They are keen to have the reassurance that everything will be covered and it saves the time and effort of sourcing and preparing their own materials. It may also be a tempting prospect to think that it might make the Adviser happy. Some packages supply tests and marked assignments which offer the advantage of some input from an independent adult. These factors may be very compelling, particularly for parents who have undertaken home education in desperation after problems in school. They may feel very nervous about taking on the responsibility especially in the early stages of education at home. They may make the assumption that a model which has many of the characteristics of learning at school is likely to be successful.

A purchased curriculum may be fine for you even though it may be an expensive option. It may be helpful if you are travelling abroad and if you are likely to have difficulty obtaining materials. But there may be some disadvantages. The layout and presentation of most courses are predictable. Some children may like to know what to expect but others may soon tire of the approach and lose interest in the material. This method of study suits some children but not others and you might find yourself committed for months ahead to a course which your child loathes. Older children who are used to school may be able to manage the demands of a correspondence course but younger ones may find it too much. If a child has been under stress at school or if motivation has been damaged it would be unwise to start work on a commercially prepared curriculum at an early stage.

Employing tutors for the entire education is not an option for most families because of the cost, but some people decide to pay for some outside help if their child wants to study a subject that is unfamiliar to them. It is worth noting that some professional private tutors are not used to working with home educators and they may not know much about it. Most of their work is geared towards supplementing the education for children who are behind in school or who are preparing intensively for exams.

If you are planning to enlist the help of other people, it is important to bear in mind the whole issue of child safety and take sensible precautions. It is a sad and unpleasant fact that there are a few individuals who do take advantage of children in situations where the opportunity presents itself.

Parents may want some support for subjects like languages, music or maths at secondary level, but there is no need to employ someone with a teaching qualification. An informal arrangement made with a person who has a particular skill may work very well on a one-to-one basis. Some families have found that university students are very helpful and sympathetic tutors.

A semi-formal approach

Christine and Tim began home education by following a school model, but moved away from this naturally as their work progressed:

> We took Adam out of school when he was 10 because of bullying. He had been attacked both in school and on the way to school and the last straw came one day when he came home with a broken arm and lumps of his hair pulled out. The bullies were known but the school didn't seem to be able to do anything about it. He was afraid to go back, so while he was at home recovering from this we wrote to the school and told them that we would be educating him at home. We intended to keep him out for his last year and send him to the local secondary school where our daughter goes, but when the time came we found that the boys who had tormented him would all be at the same school anyway. There was nowhere else for him to go as the nearest secondary school with places was miles away in the next town.
>
> At first we stuck closely to the national curriculum as we thought he was going back to school. We used to work in the mornings at his school subjects and we found that we could cover everything comfortably by lunchtime. We divided up the morning into 'lessons' as we didn't want him to get too far away from the pattern of school. As far as we could, we got books which were similar to the ones that he would have been using in school, and we would read through a chapter at a time and do the exercises at the end. We did history and geography projects like the ones they were doing in school, and in the afternoons we made models and drew pictures and did the creative parts of the projects.

As time went on we found other things that we wanted to look into, so we began to move away from the national curriculum. He started to learn French but after a while he decided that he wasn't enjoying it, so we gave that up. We have tried lots of things including astronomy and geology and Dutch! Now he is 13 we are following a maths course and using Key Stage 3 materials in some other subjects. We don't have a timetable any more but at the weekend we work out a rough amount which we have to cover in each subject per week. He is very interested in his computer and he spends a lot of time on it, and he wants to do GCSE Information Technology first.

Semi-formal approaches make it possible to benefit from the advantages of both informal and structured learning. Some structured, formal learning may be helpful especially if the child has been withdrawn from school and particularly in the secondary years. You can decide upon a level of structure which is appropriate to your situation and to the age and interests of your child. Even if you are starting at the beginning with a 5-year-old, you may feel more comfortable with a certain amount of order to the days and weeks ahead. It is entirely a matter of personal choice.

Some planning will be needed, and this will range from a set of general objectives over a period of time to a detailed week planner laying out the subjects to be covered each day. Also, if your children are interested in leisure courses, clubs or social activities it may be necessary to plan and budget for these in order to safeguard both the work plan and the family finances. To determine the level of structure which is needed, the semi-formal educator would perhaps ask some of these questions:

- What do I want to help the children to learn in the next three months/six months/year?
- Do we need to work on basic skills to start with?
- What strengths and weaknesses do the children have?
- What subject areas/topics/new knowledge do I want to introduce them to and when?
- Are we going to work with the different subject areas or are we going to work on different topics – or a mixture of both?
- What help do they need in order to make progress in the areas which interest them?
- How can I help them to manage their time and develop their learning skills?
- Do we need help from other people for certain subjects?
- Do we need to use correspondence courses for some subjects?

- Are there any part-time courses at the further education college which might be helpful?
- How will we organize our work on a daily basis?

Semi-formal methods do have the advantage of allowing the learner to have a considerable input into the educational arrangements, while parents are able to use their experience and organizational skills to help the child to get the most out of the home education.

When you are starting out you may find it necessary to make changes and adjustments as you go. You may need to try things out and you should be prepared to drop them if they are not suitable. It may be difficult at first to estimate the amount of work that the child will be able to cover and you will also need time to assess the level of the work required. Books and materials that are not challenging enough are unrewarding and the child will soon become demotivated if they are too difficult.

An informal approach

Fleur and Jonathan had a passionate commitment to informal learning from the beginning:

We have two children, Aster aged 9 and Calum who is 7. We decided not to send them to school when Aster was 4 as we had several friends living in our village who educated their children from home. We very much wanted our children to learn when they were ready, without coercion or pressure. We believe firmly that children learn best when they need to know something, so we are here as facilitators rather than teachers. They learn a terrific amount from their own world: they help to keep the animals, they are involved with the work on the smallholding and Aster has her own patch of garden too. They are very active and they are always out of doors. They build dens and they have a tree-house where they spend a lot of time when the weather is warm.

Indoors we have plenty of books, art and craft materials, educational resources and the computer. They can choose to use these when they want to. Aster loves drawing and modelling and right now she is finding out a lot about birds. Calum is interested in numbers, especially measurements for building work and calculating the amount of feed that we have to buy for the animals. He has his own chickens and he sells the eggs to friends. Both children love us to read to them. We don't plan their education and we don't try to 'teach' them anything – we just live each day as it comes.

Informal approaches require parents to have the courage to let go and the ability to trust their children to share responsibility for their own learning. Understandably, most parents try to ensure progress in literacy and basic numeracy while presenting lots of opportunities and choices which allow the child to decide on the rest of the education.

Undoubtedly a 'hands-off' approach suits the learning style of some children. It enables them to find out how to learn and how to manage their time, and it gives them the opportunity to pursue their interests in depth if they wish. Sometimes young people may become exceptionally good at a particular subject or skill because they have the chance to give it priority in their life.

If you are starting out with a 5-year-old who has never been to school, it would be possible to view home education simply as a continuation of the natural and unforced learning which occurs in the pre-school years. You may find that the process evolves into something different as your children grow older and their needs change. We have talked to quite a few families who began in a totally spontaneous and informal fashion and moved on to become more structured as the home education progressed. We have also witnessed the opposite effect taking place.

If this approach is right for you, there are many potential advantages. Informal education gives families the freedom to make the most of the learning opportunities that arise naturally from daily life. The need for planning is removed and the home educating parent is able to accompany the child in the adventure of learning as a spontaneous activity. Conflict and the negative outcomes of constant battles over education are removed, and learning may be integrated with life. Incidentally, we have known of many young people who have received very little formal education in earlier years who have achieved success in exams once they have decided to commit themselves to formal study.

How to start? Consider how far you will take the principle of informality in education. Be consistent if you feel there are certain boundaries beyond which you cannot go. Together with your child you may decide to modify your informal approach as time goes on. Be prepared to be flexible and think about the different options and opportunities which you can offer to your learners, but don't be surprised if they choose something entirely different.

Don't expect breadth and balance in the education in the short term, as many families have reported that this only becomes noticeable after quite a long period of time. In a famous experiment which was conducted in the early twentieth century and reported in the *Canadian Medical Association Journal* (1939), Dr Clara M. Davis arranged for fifteen babies in an orphanage to select their own diets, although at that point none of them had tasted any food apart from baby milk. They could choose whatever they liked from a wide range of healthy natural foods and the experiment lasted for six years. All of the babies went on food binges, perhaps eating nothing but bananas one day and just eggs on the next. Often certain foods were avoided for a while and then eaten heartily. The foods that they ate and the quantities taken were carefully recorded. On a daily basis the diets were totally unbalanced, but somehow balance was achieved over a period of time and all the children were well nourished. None of the children had any serious illness during the experiment. Perhaps there are parallels with education here that might give us food for thought.

What are the problems? Parents find that it may be hard when they have to face questioning from others about their children's education. It may need great strength of mind to carry on if there is very little to confirm their progress to outside observers. Courage and determination may also be needed when the LEA's Adviser asks for information about your arrangements.

Before we move on we should mention autonomous learning which places the whole responsibility for learning upon the child. A small number of parents are ardent supporters of freedom in education, giving their children complete control of their own learning. Whether the child exercises freedom by doing nothing or by following a purchased curriculum, the autonomous home educator would respect the young person's decision.

Autonomy in education is sometimes a lifestyle choice which is made by parents when their children are infants. Complete freedom to choose may also be just what's needed if an older child's motivation has been damaged by bad experiences in school. Some teenagers readily accept the opportunity to be in charge of their own education but it has to be said that others find it very hard to adjust to managing their own learning after years of being in the school system.

Whether you choose a structured approach, a very informal one or something in between, one thing is certain: you will find that your ideas will change as you go ahead with home education.

Getting started

If your children are of pre-school age and you are planning to educate them at home there may be some anxious moments when 'compulsory school age' draws near. If they have attended a playgroup they may miss the activity when they leave, and they may be puzzled when all their friends disappear into school. Some families avoid playgroups for this reason and they may make determined efforts to get to know other home educators at an early stage. The national organizations provide membership lists to help with social contact, and it is worth remembering that most other families are just as keen as you are to make a social life for their children! There are also many other clubs, classes and groups for young children in the community, so it's a good idea to plan ahead and get information about local activities which will follow on from pre-school groups.

If you have made a firm decision to educate your 5-year-old at home, what do you do if the child then demands to go to school? Some people would argue that the parent should always respect the child's wishes in the matter of their education. Others would point out that very young children aren't capable of making an informed decision as they have neither the breadth of experience nor the ability to conceptualize the reality of ten years at school. First of all, try to find out the reasoning behind the request. It may surprise you! One child thought that going to school was a one-off event and once you had been you didn't go again. Another had been used to seeing the children running around in the playground at break time and thought that this was all you did in school. And one very small person was consumed with the desire for a fluorescent yellow school bag (a request that was easily granted!).

Making the transition from school to home
If you are withdrawing a child from school you may be in crisis already. Older children may be desperate to get out of school and they may be angry, emotionally low and depressed. Once the pressure of school is removed they may be uncooperative and demotivated. They may want to stay in bed all day, go out all day or watch television all day. There may be a period of recovery when nothing much happens. Writing about their experiences or depicting them in artwork may help some young people. Looking at new subjects and interests may help, and a complete change of educational approach often enables them to start afresh without the associations of school. You will need time to try things out and space to sort out the emotional problems as well. Whether they are 6 or 16 the young person will have to adjust to a new routine and get used to an entirely different educational experience. This takes time, so don't expect too much at first.

Waiting for a school place
Increasing numbers of parents are turning to home education as a temporary measure when they find that they cannot get a place for their child in a suitable school. Popular schools have long waiting lists and it may be some time before your child's name comes to the top of

the list. In the meantime there are things that you can do to help your child to fit in when the time comes. It may be helpful to have a daily routine and a subject-based approach, but you are unlikely to need to spend as many hours on home education as there are in the school day. Home education is very intensive so it is a good idea to allow plenty of time for breaks and varied activities.

If you are able to make contact with families who already have children of the same age in the proposed school you may be able to gain useful information about textbooks, topics and subjects studied. Sometimes staff at the school may be willing to give some details of the work which is to be covered, but they are under no obligation to do so.

Giving information to the LEA

If you withdraw a child from school, the LEA is likely to contact you for information when they hear about it. As the procedure is not specified in law there are local variations, and we recommend that you join HEAS or EO for advice and information. The experience of three home educating parents will give some idea of what you might expect. Sally explains:

> The education welfare officer telephoned me to ask if she could come and see us about Natalie's education. She explained that she was contacting us to make sure that we were aware of our duty to educate Natalie and also to tell us about the availability of places in other schools in the area. The visit was brief and the education welfare officer said that it was not her job to ask us for details of what Natalie was learning, as the Adviser would be doing that later on. She seemed quite interested in the idea of home education. It must be quite a change from dealing with truants, I think.

In most areas a representative from the LEA's Inspection and Advisory Service will contact you thereafter. Again, the procedure varies considerably in different parts of the country. Another parent, Nick, remembers his family's first visit from the Adviser:

> Several months after we began home educating we heard from the LEA that Mr Smith would like to come and make an appraisal of our home education. We agreed to the visit as we didn't mind him coming and it seemed to be the easiest way of explaining what we were doing. We got all my son's files out and tidied them up before the visit, and we put all the books and CD-ROMs out on the table. We had been keeping a diary of his reading books and we had made notes on our outings and visits and on the

practical work that we had done. Mr Smith asked my son to read to him and he talked to him about some of the topics that we had started. He suggested a few related ideas that we could follow up and he seemed quite happy with what we had done. He was a bit taken aback when he realized that we didn't have everything planned in advance, but we explained that we didn't work like that. Home education is very different from school and I think he's still getting used to that idea.

My advice is that you must be certain and positive about your approach as it's quite difficult for Advisers to judge an entire education on the basis of an hour's visit and some pieces of work. If you seem to be tentative or unsure it might appear to them that you don't know what you're doing.

Some forms of home education are easier for Advisers to assess than others. Sarah had chosen to educate her children informally:

We found it was a problem that a lot of what we had done didn't leave any 'evidence' so there was nothing to show for it. Mrs Jones was polite and respectful but when she looked at what we had to show her we could tell that it wasn't what she was expecting. We had taken advice from HEAS so we knew that the LEA couldn't insist that we change our education in order to suit the inspection, so we had a frank discussion with Mrs Jones about the way forward. We had to negotiate mutually acceptable ways of providing information to the LEA so that she knew what to expect in future.

It may be helpful to contact other families in your area to ask about their relationships with the LEA, but remember that it's important to keep an open mind as every family's experience is different. HEAS and EO will be able to help you with information and advice about the LEA and if you join the organizations they should be able to put you in touch with other families.

CHAPTER 5

Learning at home in the primary years

Home educators are able to decide on the kind of education that they want for their children. There are no subjects which are compulsory at home, and there are many different ways of teaching and learning.

The word 'curriculum' means the content and form of the education. It need not imply a structured provision. Your home education may be as informal or as structured as you wish. The curriculum may be a broad outline of the subjects or topics that you have chosen or a set of specific objectives but you don't have to put it in writing for the LEA.

Every family has their own priorities and every experience of home education will have a different balance and emphasis. Some families integrate all their learning without dividing it into 'subjects'. Others focus on the skills of literacy and numeracy and organize the rest of their learning into topics. And then there are those families who like to plan their home education according to the traditional subject divisions.

Key Stage 1	Age 5 up to age 7	(Years 1 and 2)
Key Stage 2	Age 7 up to age 11	(Years 3 to 6)
Key Stage 3	Age 11 up to age 14	(Years 7 to 9)
Key Stage 4	Age 14 up to age 16	(Years 10 and 11)

Table 5.1 *The Key Stages of the national curriculum*

Table 5.1 is included here because educational books and materials often refer to the Key Stages and the school years but parents who don't have children in the school system often find these references confusing. The Key Stages and their levels are all to do with the measurement of children's progress, but they are not relevant at home. Among home educators, there is a great variation in the ages at which children develop skills and it's natural that some children should make progress more rapidly than others. Some learners are ahead in some areas and not so far advanced in others. This doesn't present any problems at home as children don't have to be assessed according to the objectives of the national curriculum. There is no pressure upon them to achieve certain things by a certain age.

Beginning home education with your 5-year-old

If your child has never been to school you can integrate education into life without making a big thing of 'school'. If you wish, you can continue with the established pre-school learning pattern which is already part of life. As we discussed in Chapter 3, some families continue learning informally for years in ways which evolve naturally from the pre-school experience.

Others like to mark the transition to a new stage in their children's life, celebrating the beginning of home education perhaps with a cake and a present of a special new exercise book and a set of coloured pencils or felt tip pens ... or their very own table and chair. Some children attach great importance to a 'rite of passage' of this kind and they are proud to be included in the grown-up activity of learning, especially if they have older brothers or sisters.

You may like to take each day as it comes, or you might want to start by having a time each day for sitting down together for educational activities. These could include reading together, drawing, counting, playing games and puzzles and making things. You can progress gradually to more extended activities which build on the child's developing skills.

Many families have a child of school age and a baby or toddler around as well. If you have a baby or a younger child who still sleeps during the day, you could aim to use this time for learning with the older child. Or you could give the younger one something absorbing to do so that you can spend some time with the older one. Useful entertainments include a video or audiotape, a favourite programme on television, playdough, a bag of special things which only comes out while you are with the older child or some favourite toys and games that are kept out of circulation for the rest of the time. If you end with a diversion such as a drink and a biscuit or a walk or similar, you can usually quietly remove the activity so that it stays fresh and special for as long as possible.

Sometimes it may not work if the younger child won't be diverted but try not to get irritated and anxious if this happens. It won't hurt if you miss your time with the older one sometimes. The older child is learning a lot from talking, listening, questioning, observing and comparing, and the distraction of the younger child or children won't last for very long. Learning individually at home is very intensive, so you can do a lot in a short time. Don't be daunted by the concept of 'full-time' education. It doesn't mean that you should sit your child down to work for the entire school day. This would be a recipe for disaster when you're learning at home!

Enjoyment, praise and gentle encouragement are the keys to successful learning.

Learning at home in the primary years

What follows in this and the next two chapters is not a recommended method and it is not intended to be prescriptive. It is not designed to be a complete curriculum in all subjects for children of all ages. Although reference is made to school subjects these chapters are not meant to be a guide to the national curriculum. There are no boundaries to learning at home. The ideas below are offered to help parents who don't know where to start, and they may serve as a guide to help parents to think about the task ahead of them. Under the subject headings you will find a range of favourite activities and suggestions from parents to give you ideas in the different subject areas, plus comments and hints on topics and approaches that have worked for some families. You'll notice that we've given a large amount of attention to literacy and numeracy in our comments. Project work for both younger and older children is discussed in Chapter 6.

Just for comparison we'll mention that the national curriculum, which doesn't apply to home education, has the following compulsory subjects in school at Key Stages 1 and 2: English, maths, science, history, geography, religious education, design and technology, information and communication technology (ICT), art and design, music, physical education. Many schools also teach personal, social and health education and citizenship but these are not compulsory. Most home educators would not regard these as separate subjects as they occur so naturally in daily life at home.

Study of foreign languages is not part of the national curriculum until Key Stage 3, but we've included some ideas on languages as many home educating families like to begin language study with younger children. We have included comments on the most relevant aspects of design and technology and ICT under the headings 'Technology' and 'Familiarity with computers', and history, geography and religious education are discussed together as 'Humanities'. Ideas for physical activity are included in Chapter 8.

English

The development of the child's skills in reading, writing, speaking and listening is crucial to future educational progress in all areas of the curriculum, and practising these skills may take up quite a lot of time in the primary years.

Reading
Laying the foundations for reading begins at an early stage long before children reach school age. All the things which parents do anyway in the pre-school years are important in preparing for reading. Most parents spend time naming things, looking at picture books, reading stories, playing with alphabet letters and relating the pictures to words. They write individual letters and well-known words, including the names of family members and pets, and encourage the child to copy them. Children are surrounded by words everywhere in daily life in addition to text in books, magazines and so on. Also, children see other people around them all the time who are reading for various reasons. For most children, literacy is part of everyday living.

Through these daily experiences and informal activities children acquire the basic knowledge and skills necessary for competence in reading: recognizing letters and their sounds, knowing that words are made out of letters, knowing common sequences of letters and realizing that words go across the page from left to right. In homes where people read for pleasure children will want to read for themselves, and later they will see the usefulness of reading as a means of getting information.

At what age should your child be reading? Children who are educated at home learn to read at widely differing ages. Some will be fluent at 3 years while others may be around 11 before they are readers. At school late readers are at a disadvantage and they may fall behind as a result, but children who are educated at home don't have the same problem. Reading may be delayed because they are learning all sorts of things in other ways, particularly if there is a parent who is always on hand to read to them and to answer their questions. A child who finds that the process of acquiring reading skills is difficult and laborious will take longer to get there. Learning to read may not be a priority for a child who is interested in physical or outdoor activities, or who is busy with artistic and creative tasks.

Whatever the reason, literacy doesn't have the urgency at home that it does in school, at least not for the child. Research suggests that up to one in five home educated children may not start reading until they are at least 8 years old (see Thomas, 2000, p. 103), and the findings indicate that the age at which reading begins, within certain limits, doesn't really matter. At school, though, it's well established that the reading gap widens for poor readers in school as they grow older. Morag Stuart says: 'My research carries the rather depressing message that as you start, so you finish. The gap between good and poor readers widens as time goes on. Make sure you give your children a good start' (quoted in McMillan and Leslie, 1998).

Which way of teaching reading is best? There are many different schemes and methods and there is heated debate among educationalists about their relative merits. From time to time one approach is hailed as the definitive method which will ensure success for all children. We would like to sound a note of caution. Despite the claims which are made about some methods, no reading strategy will guarantee success for every child as they are all individuals. We cannot say: 'Follow this method and your child will learn to read.' At home, you can experiment to find out which method or combination of methods will be most suitable for your child, and this is something which teachers cannot do in school.

Methods of teaching reading are designed to help teachers in the classroom to achieve the greatest degree of success with the greatest number of children. Broadly speaking, there are two kinds of approach: one is based on building up sounds into words (phonics based) and the other is visual (look and say, or whole language methods). You will find books in the library which give explanations of the various methods which will help you to decide on a strategy. You may find that you start off with one approach and it becomes necessary to drop it and move to something else. You may wish to use elements of several methods.

Many parents assume that reading schemes are necessary because they are used widely in schools. These consist of a series of books which start with picture books and become gradually more complex in their vocabulary and sentence structure. Although reading schemes may be useful in the classroom they aren't essential for individual learning at home. Pamela found a reading scheme helpful:

We began by using a reading scheme because a teacher friend passed on books that were being discarded at school. It was quite good but it would have been too expensive for one family buying it new. We wouldn't have bought it ourselves. Frances was a relatively late reader but she has always loved books. We taught her some of the letter sounds but not very systematically, and she just picked up reading from recognizing the words as we read to her. Some favourite books were read over and over again, and I'm sure this helped a lot.

Unlike Pamela, Joan used a mixture of approaches:

We found that reading grew naturally out of our child's interest in books through being read to. We taught her using a mixture of phonics and whole words, and we didn't use a reading scheme. We just looked out for simple books that she liked. We started by learning the sounds of the letters and the combinations, using cardboard letters and making words. We discovered letters all over the place, not just in books! We made our own little books of a few pages each using very simple sentences made up from the words we had learned.

Some children learn to read at home without being taught directly at all. This may happen where there is an older sibling who is being taught to read, and the younger ones absorb much by listening and watching the process. You can extend and develop their skills by reading with them, and you may decide either to introduce systematic methods at this point or to continue with this informal 'apprenticeship'.

Some families prefer to use a structured method of teaching reading, and young children may see a phonics-based approach as a game. Once they have learned the different letter-sounds and the additional combinations of letters you can have fun making up words with them. Choose 'regular' words at first that sound as they are spelt, and draw their attention to these words in their reading.

Whatever method you use it's crucial to be relaxed and unhurried. Progress may be slow simply because some children take much longer than others to get going on reading. When children are learning successfully in other respects and there are no medical problems or special needs which might be associated with reading difficulties, it's likely that they will read when they are ready. If you suspect that there might be a serious problem it would be sensible to seek help. Try to avoid anxiety as this will make the problem worse. It's worth seeking a range of views before you do anything. You may wish to obtain advice from an educational psychologist or from a reading specialist, but do bear in mind that there is no agreement among experts about the best time for this. Some experts maintain that early assessment is vital while others say that it is a mistake to assess children until they are at least 14.

Writing

Writing is next in importance after reading, but it's not nearly as vital at home as it is in school. Children at school spend large amounts of time writing as it's used as a means of facilitating communication between one teacher and around thirty pupils, in order to consolidate learning and to demonstrate the pupils' understanding. At home you can talk to your child to find out whether or not they have understood a topic. Written work in the classroom provides evidence of learning and it also helps in classroom management; children who are writing are occupied and quiet. At home you don't need to get children to write at length on a daily basis to be satisfied that they are learning or in order to control them. Instead you can concentrate on writing for its primary purposes of communication and creative expression.

The age at which children become ready to write varies considerably when they are learning at home. Some children may start early and they may enjoy expressing themselves in writing, but others might not start writing until they are much older than the school norm. This is not a cause for concern at home as the amount of time which is devoted to all aspects of writing in school is only necessary within a school situation. Over the years many home educators have found that their children have developed excellent writing skills in spite of the fact that they have done far less writing than would have been required in school.

As with reading, the foundations of writing are laid in the early years when children discover the joys of making marks with pencils and crayons. Much scribbling and drawing lead on naturally to the acquisition of writing skills as the child's fine motor skills develop. There are many activities involving the child's fingers and thumb which refine the skills needed for handwriting, including picking up small items, doing jigsaws, doing up buttons, manipulating toys and many other things which occur naturally from day to day.

There are different approaches to teaching writing. Some parents like to teach the skills formally, perhaps using workbooks for the child which contain exercises to develop pre-writing skills, including joining dots and making letter shapes. Other parents take a very relaxed view of writing, making the assumption that their children will come to writing eventually once they have learned to read. The critical factor is that the child should be ready and willing to make a start on writing, as it would be damaging in the long run to try to force a reluctant learner to write.

Margaret remembers how writing was learned very naturally in their family:

Ben learned to hold a pencil from watching his sister in church. We used to take a bag of crayons and paper for Natalie when she was 5 to keep her quiet, and he wanted to join in as well. He soon learned to hold the crayons with two fingers and thumb just like she did, and he loved scribbling and colouring. When he was 4 we showed him how to print his name and we began to teach him how to print his letters. We taught the upper-case ones first as they are easier to form and not so confusing. Natalie taught him most of the lower-case ones, and he's now ready to print short sentences and titles for his pictures.

Rose encountered resistance after a good start:

Justin began writing when he was 5 and once he could print his letters he used to love to write pretend shopping lists and menus for his café. He would write on anything, especially if it already had writing on it. We found triangular pencil grips very useful – we got them from an early learning shop. We got on well with writing until he was about 7 but gradually it became a bit of a chore for him. I didn't want to force it so we stopped altogether for a while. It was summer and we were busy with lots of outdoor learning. Eventually we tried again, just a little bit at first, and he soon remembered. We've found some workbooks that he likes and he does a couple of pages a day.

Sarah's daughter likes to write poems:

Emily (9 years) enjoys drawing pictures and writing stories and poems. A favourite way of starting a poem off is for us to write an interesting word in capital letters down the page. Then she writes each line of her poem across the page, starting each line with a letter from the word.

Claire's family has a diary:

Sometimes we keep a family diary where we all take turns in thinking up what to put in for the day. We write in it after dinner if we think there's anything interesting to record. We don't do it every day. The boys (8 and 10) take it in turns to be 'scribe' and it's one piece of writing that they always like doing.

There are lots of other ideas which may help to get your child interested in writing. Some children love drawing pictures and you could suggest that they might give them titles. As you go on these may be expanded to a sentence or two about each picture. Sometimes parents encourage their child to have a special book for writing, and children often take great delight in seeing their drawings and writing building up as the weeks go by. Writing need not take place every day and children do remember even if there has been a gap, as Rose noted in the extract quoted above.

Some parents become anxious if the writing is very untidy and the letters are poorly formed, but this nearly always resolves itself with practice and it's important to be very positive and full of praise for the child's achievements. Some people like to use special handwriting paper printed with extra lines, but this may be demoralizing for children whose coordination has not yet developed sufficiently to enable them to keep their letters between the lines. Forming the letters may be practised as a separate skill until it becomes easy, and you can have fun inventing silly sentences for them to write down. Invariably they come up with some of their own once you have given them the idea! Word games, spelling games, crosswords, Scrabble, wordsearches and all sorts of written activities are often enjoyed by younger children especially if you do them together.

You could cut out pictures from magazines and catalogues and ask the child to use them to tell a story; you could write the story down yourself in the early stages of learning. You could try making posters using pictures, photos and drawings which are accompanied by a few words, phrases or sentences. See if the child would like to write some captions to accompany a selection of your holiday photographs or pictures of a special occasion. The pictures and the captions could then be mounted on sheets of card and displayed. Grannies and aunties always welcome these as presents, and their enthusiasm is very encouraging for the child.

Composition in writing is a separate part of the process which may be developed naturally and easily by lots of talking, listening, telling stories, discussing experiences, describing events, explaining things and making jokes. Children love to hear about your own experiences when you were a child, especially if they involve humour, surprise or a twist at the end of the story. The skill of selecting information and arranging it in a sequence is developed by listening and by talking. Children who can tell a story clearly and put the events in the correct order will find both creative and factual writing much easier later on.

Speaking and listening
Speaking and listening are just as important as reading and writing, and all four skills work together. Lorraine comments:

> We encourage the children to listen as well as to talk. We get story tapes from the library and we listen to some of the schools programmes on the radio, but we don't have a television. We've noticed that both telling stories and listening to them are helping both their reading and their writing.

Maths
Parents of pre-school children often do a lot of essential maths activities with them without really noticing. Counting and talking about

numbers is part of life at home with a pre-schooler; sharing things is part of family life; sorting out the laundry, the knives and forks and the toys are daily activities; counting songs, nursery rhymes and poems are time-honoured ways of entertaining and amusing young children. You can build on these kinds of activities to make a good start in maths and there's no need to wait until your child is 5. As with reading and writing, it's sensible to continue at the child's pace and to build on the skills and understanding which have been acquired during the pre-school years.

Maths worries many parents, especially those who were not good at it when they were at school. It's likely that you will have forgotten some maths but you can learn as you go along. Some parents find themselves getting a better grasp of maths than they ever had while they were at school themselves. When you begin maths with a younger child, you have the chance to start again from basics. There are many workbooks and courses for primary maths which are easily available at a low cost, and in addition to using these materials you can encourage your child to learn maths informally through everyday activities. Practical maths is invaluable as an aid to understanding abstract mathematical concepts and it also means that learning maths will have real meaning.

At home you can avoid unnecessary repetition which some children find unbearably tedious when they are learning maths at school. Repetition in the classroom is justified by teachers as a means of en-suring that all the pupils have mastered the topic fully. Of course, some children require a great deal of practice in order to grasp a concept or a method of working, but others pick up the idea quickly and they are turned off by an overdose of the topic. Home educators have the realization that once you have understood something, that's enough. You can tailor the exercises to the child's understanding and it doesn't matter if it's forgotten; you can revise it when you need it next time.

Lesley recalls maths with her family in the early years:

We played lots of card games and board games when our children were young. We played snap, snakes and ladders, ludo, dominoes and lotto games. We went shopping and counted the change. They counted the pocket money in the piggy bank. They used to count the railings and the flagstones and the lampposts and the front doors ... .We did lots of things informally until the eldest was about 7, then we looked for a course as we wanted to make sure that we didn't miss out anything important. It was a standard course in eight books that was designed for schools, and it lasted us through until the secondary stage. We used the bits of the course that we needed and we left out topics that we had covered already.

Ella had problems with materials:

I bought a maths course as I thought it would be worth it for two children, but it just didn't suit both of them. My daughter liked the course and worked through it, but when my son came to it he didn't like it at all. I didn't want to put him off maths altogether so we used several other textbooks and took parts out of all of them. It was rather awkward at times but you do have to be flexible when you educate children at home.

Sue links maths with other subjects:

My son is very keen on maths puzzles and tricks. We have also just finished looking at maths in the time of the Romans and the Egyptians. We have had lots of fun looking at Roman numerals, tiles, patterns and symmetry and we have also been making pyramids. The links between maths, art and history really make it come alive for both of us.

Julian and Sophie favoured an informal approach:

We decided not to follow a curriculum in maths as we wanted to work with subjects that occurred naturally as we went along. We worked on mathematical topics as they were needed in our daily routine through making things, cooking, gardening, building, shopping and in the daily round on the farm. Telling the time, weighing and measuring, counting, estimating, money, capacity and fractions have all been covered in real situations first, then when we sit down in the afternoons we help them to record what they've learned. We keep all their records and discoveries in scrap books so they can look back and refresh their memories. Everything we've done so far has come from real life, so that they can see why we need these skills.

Clement compares the home with the classroom:

As a maths teacher turned home educator, I've been struck by how successful maths at home seems to be among the families I have met. When I was teaching I came across so many children who hated maths and said that they were no good at it, but home educated children don't seem to have the same attitude. I've seen genuine fear and anxiety about the subject among pupils at school, but children who are taught at home don't seem to be daunted by it. Families that I know often do lots of practical maths which gives the children confidence, and of course they can work at their own pace at home without feeling intimidated by pupils who are catching on more quickly than they are.

Home educators have one overriding advantage which applies to maths as well as to other areas of knowledge. All too often in school children struggle and fail to make progress because they don't understand a basic concept. When your child is learning with you on a one-to-one basis at home, any misunderstandings or problems may be sorted out as soon as they arise.

Science

What does science mean to you? Perhaps something similar to the views of these parents? 'Messing about with chemicals ... '; 'The unique smell of the lab ... '; 'Lots of formulae that were impossible to remember ... '; 'Bunsen burners and rubber bungs ... '; 'The science teachers in their white coats who inhabited a different world from the rest of the staff ... '. Many home educating parents think of science in terms of their experiences in their own schooldays when the subject wasn't taught before secondary level and it didn't exist outside the science lab anyway. Some parents are not confident about helping their children to learn science at home, even at primary level. It's a pity that their own education has left them with these misconceptions and uncertainties. Primary science is about awakening a sense of wonder in young children together with a desire to find out about the world 'scientifically', that is, by observation, experiment and analysis. As these parents found, it's crucial to foster the child's interest and curiosity in the early years as a foundation for a good attitude to science later on.

Charlotte says:

Science begins when children are interested in their surroundings and when they start to ask 'Why ... ?' When we stopped to think about it, we could see that we had covered an awful lot of science in the primary years just by responding to their questions. They were very excited by visits to the Science Museum. We had several books of science experiments, some of which came from the Science Museum's bookshop. We tested things with magnets, we collected oxygen from pondweed, we kept tadpoles until they turned into frogs, we looked at roots and rhizomes and tubers, we kept weather records, we looked at snowflakes through a magnifying glass, we made a sand and gravel filter for cleaning muddy water, we watched butterflies and birds and badgers and all sorts of animals, we collected fossils, we worked out the age of hedges from the species in them, we made solar-powered toys and wondered at wind farms ... but when we set out to do experiments they often went wrong! But there was something to be learned from the failures, too, as we would then have to find out why the expected result didn't happen.

Mike remembers planning science activities:

We're not scientists ourselves so we read up as much as we could on scientific ideas when we first started home education. We planned a list of topics including animal, vegetable and mineral, the weather, energy and moving things about, the solar system, our bodies, the sea and the four seasons. We helped them with different ways of keeping records of what we discovered. We tried to develop a scientific approach so that they could learn the skills of measuring, describing, predicting, observing, comparing, finding patterns by experiment and identifying variables. There were masses of things to do and we learnt a lot with the children along the way.

Hugh and Julia adopted an integrated approach to science:

We see science as something that should be integrated with our other learning and with daily life, and we don't have a science curriculum as such. Plenty of science topics have just arisen out of a chance remark or a child's observation which we have followed up as an opportunity for learning. For instance, one of the children became interested in a picture of the sun with a face on from an old clockface. This led to all sorts of things including investigations of shadows, sundials, burning holes in paper with a magnifying glass, light and how it travels through space, the size of the sun, sunlight and plants, poems and artwork about the sun, solar power and solar panels, the myth of Daedalus and Icarus, sunspots and the dangers of sunburn.

We also have a children's science encyclopaedia which is a wonderful source of information and ideas. All the children have enjoyed just reading it and finding out all sorts of scientific facts from it. We often do the home experiments from it as one-off activities because they look interesting. It may seem rather a 'rag-bag' approach, but we've found that it works. The order of our discoveries doesn't seem to matter because they remember all sorts of things and put them together as they make sense of them.

Sometimes new home educators think that science is a very specialized subject that must require training and expertise. The most important qualifications for home scientists, though, are enthusiasm, resourcefulness and the desire to investigate.

Languages
Some people leave the study of foreign languages until the secondary years, but you can start whenever you wish. Some teachers say that early experience of languages helps children to be successful later on. Undoubtedly it helps if you have a reason for the study of a particular language, for instance if you have a friend or relative living abroad with whom you correspond. This will bring the language to life for your child.

May explains how her family became interested in languages:

We decided to look at some European countries to get an idea of what life is like for children there. The whole idea came about after Jamie read a book in the library about a cow who fell into a canal in Holland. This little story gave rise to lots of curiosity about canals, Dutch cheese, what it's like to live in a country with no hills (we live in the Lake District!) and what the towns and houses and churches and schools and shops look like. We have a Dutch friend who taught us some simple things to say and showed us her photos of her home town. We now have a scrapbook with some postcards from our friend, some labels from different cheeses, and lots of pictures of everyday things with the Dutch words written underneath. Then we started wondering what our everyday things would be called in other languages and our project took off. We are looking at Spain at the moment and it will be good to find out about some other countries while Jamie's interest lasts.

Anna seized on an interest and made it happen:

The boys decided that they wanted to learn Japanese so I fixed up for a Japanese lady to come and see us once a week and I thought I'd do some too. I didn't know how long it would last but I thought we'd give it a try. After all, if they do keep it up a knowledge of Japanese is very useful in the business world. After a while a completely unexpected opportunity arose for us to visit Japan and we spent a couple of weeks there. It was terrific and we have made some good contacts. We keep in touch by email and fax.

Jane has good reasons for an unusual choice of language:

Home education does give families the chance to study languages which are not on the school curriculum, and for us that's a good thing. Danny's father is from Kenya and although he doesn't see him very often I do want him to retain some links with his father's culture. He wants to learn about his native language and I'm starting him off with what I know until I can find someone to teach him.

Sharon wanted to learn alongside her children:

We thought that it would be good for them to start a language early, so we listened to tapes of French songs to start them off. I remember some French from my schooldays, and we had a couple of day trips across to France to inspire them a bit. It's easy at first as you can get quite a long way by using beginners' French materials from any bookshop and with a good dictionary you can make lots of word cards and learn the vocabulary. Then we found a lovely French course for children in three books which had lots of exercises for them to do, and a tape to accompany it. I can see that we will be able to keep going until secondary level with the materials which we have got, and I plan to go to evening classes in French soon so I can keep ahead.

Hilde's family is bilingual:

We speak English and German in our house, and we have five children. They have never been to school and I am very glad! They all spoke more German than English when they were not yet 5 years old. Now they speak English also and they write it but they don't write much German yet. If they had been in school they would not have kept up with both their languages. We do most of our home school through German and my family sends us magazines and children's books and videos and school books. We are pleased that they can work this way without having trouble to understand at school.

Humanities

The main areas are history, geography, religious education, current affairs and social studies. There are many different ways of dealing with 'people studies' at home. You could treat each area as a separate branch of knowledge or you might view everything as interrelated. You could guide your children's understanding through conversations as the different issues arise, or you might like to develop these issues into topics or projects when their imagination is fired by something. Alternatively you could plan a series of topics to cover different but interrelated areas. Or you could plan work in the separate subjects of history, geography and so on, deciding on the main principles that you would like them to grasp at this stage of their learning.

Jenny believes in an integrated and informal approach:

We don't plan work at all in these areas. The children are full of curiosity about their world, other people and their ways and we find that hardly a day goes by without several issues arising which could be classified as 'humanities'. They watch a certain amount of television and this gives them glimpses of other countries and other people's ways of life. Life itself raises so many questions as we get on with the business of living it – issues of homelessness, rich and poor people, traffic congestion and public transport, building big new supermarkets which affect the town's shops, population issues and so on – and these are just some of the matters arising from going shopping!

The children are very interested in their own history and that of our family, so we see no need to study history formally yet. Within the past six months we have visited Dover Castle, Framlingham Castle, the Tower of London, Hastings and the area around it, Kew Gardens, Hampton Court and a variety of museums. Sometimes we do a project if a particular issue grabs their attention, filling a scrapbook with photos, postcards, pieces from the guide book and some written work.

Some structure is important to Helen and her family:

We do history, geography and Bible studies mainly through topics which we have planned just to make sure that the children cover the essential groundwork in each subject. We decided that our aims for primary history would be for them to have a basic outline knowledge of British history and some knowledge of past world civilizations. We have been making time-lines of the kings and queens of Britain and we have looked at China and the story of Silk, the stories of Ancient Greece, the Romans, the Normans, the Black Death, the Great Fire of London, the Age of the Explorers, the Making of America, Farms and Factories and the Victorians.

We love story-telling and we find that history fires the imagination if it's approached through story. Geography starts with us and moves outwards so that they begin to see the world as a whole of which they are a part. We like to focus on a particular country or area of the world and we always try to find as many links as possible which connect us with that country. Sometimes it may be food that we eat which comes from there, or connections through friends and relatives, films we have seen or books we have read. While we were finding out about South America, the children were very excited by Granny's stories as she had been to Brazil as a young girl. She told them about the parrot which she brought home with her which used to belong to a Brazilian sailor. The parrot used to swear roundly but fortunately no one at home understood it!

Richard's family has a global perspective:

History and geography for us are very 'hands-on' subjects. We think that our main aim in including these subjects is to help our children to understand others and to learn tolerance and respect for our world and for other people's ways of life. We're keen on conservation and a 'green' lifestyle too and we want our studies in these areas to make the children think about their individual responsibility to look after the planet on which we live. We've done projects on food, transport, recycling, energy, the history of school and the history of industry. We've also found that our reading has started off projects, based on the background of books as diverse as *The Mousehole Cat* (Nicola Bayley) and *Little House on the Prairie* (Laura Ingalls Wilder).

It is a natural part of growing up for younger children to develop a concept of time and of cause and effect, a sense of their own history, and the ability to put themselves in the place of others. These ways of thinking emerge in children whether or not they learn about history as they would in school and they form the basis of the skills needed for more formal study of the subject later on. Perhaps the most crucial factor for the study of history is a lively imagination and any activity which develops and exercises the imagination is of value to young historians. We have observed that among home educated children many develop a passion for history at quite an early age, much to the surprise of their parents. In most cases this interest seems to arise naturally and it doesn't appear to bear any relationship to the parent's skills as a teacher of history!

Religious education is an area which has a great variety of approaches. For some families it's the most important aspect of the home education and every other subject is approached through it. Some parents place great importance on the opportunity that home education gives them to impart their own beliefs to their children; many are not in favour of the multi-faith approach that is the current trend in schools. Many parents would dispute the assertion in the DfEE's publication *Learning Journey* that 'To be able to understand their own beliefs and values, children need to learn about and respond to the beliefs and values of others' (2000, p. 74). There are many ways of explaining to children that there is a need for tolerance and respect for the views of other people.

Some families find that moral and ethical issues arise out of daily life, both in the home and in the wider world. The questions which these issues generate may then be dealt with sensitively and in accordance with the family's own beliefs, and the children's faith may be nurtured according to their level of understanding. Some families don't study religion at all, and some parents feel very strongly that they should allow their children to decide on their own beliefs as they grow up. Home education caters for all these different views.

Technology

Technology is a fast-moving area of modern life and the national curriculum subjects of ICT and design and technology have become very prominent on the school timetable. It's certainly useful for children to be familiar with the major advances in technology which affect their daily lives. Young children who are learning at home tend to come across computers, the internet, scanners, fax machines and communications technology, bar codes and laser technology, computer-driven control systems and other highly sophisticated equipment in day-to-day visits to the supermarket, the library and the bank in the high street. For a clear and entertaining introduction to the subject of technology and the digital revolution, you could consult *The New Way Things Work* (Macaulay, 1998).

For younger children in addition there is a whole world of designing and making things from paper aeroplanes to bird feeders, investigating materials and their qualities, cooking and craft activities, technology challenges (try our suggestions below), problem-solving and imaginative design. Some children love the offbeat humour and rich inventiveness of W. Heath Robinson and a look at his work may well inspire them to produce some designs of their own. See if they would like to try producing a short specification and a design for an automatic cat-feeder and stroker, a machine for waking you up in the morning and getting breakfast, a mechanical laundry system (from the laundry basket to the airing cupboard) or similar. The processes may be as zany as you wish but they should be logical! Some children are fascinated by factory systems and they could try drawing a soup factory, a biscuit factory or any other process which appeals to their imagination. Such activities foster the creative thinking which inspires the technologists of the future.

Try our technology challenges:

- Can you make a tent big enough to get inside, using just sticky tape and newspaper?
- Can you make a machine for lifting an egg 30 cm off the ground using just sticky tape, newspaper and string? (Try a hardboiled one first!)
- Make a boat to carry marbles using only an A4 sheet of paper and sticky tape. What is the greatest number of marbles that it will contain without sinking?
- How long can you make an ice cube last without a freezer or a refrigerator?
- Can you make a device to enable a goldfish to swim from one container to another?
- Can you make a hot-air balloon that will rise off the ground out of doors?
- Can you design and carry out a snail race? (Do not hurt the snails!)
- How far can you move a paperclip using a balloon, a reel of thread, a drinking straw and some sticky tape?

There are no 'correct' answers to these problems and there is a range of possible approaches and solutions. It's all down to the imagination! Discuss the situations with your children and their friends and be prepared to consider even the wildest ideas.

Familiarity with computers

Although they are by no means essential for home education, computers have opened up lots of possibilities for learning and for accessing information. Susan is new to computing:

I am definitely learning with our children when it comes to computing! I notice constantly that the boys aren't intimidated by the computer at all. They learn all sorts of things just by fiddling with it and they are learning by doing. We have had some disasters and we had to reload the operating system a few weeks ago, but it was a valuable experience. We want them to become thoroughly familiar with the computer and they are acquiring some keyboard skills. They both prefer typing to writing and they will now happily produce stories and poems on the computer. They use a word processor, a touch-typing tutor, a graphics package and email. They would like to play games all the time but these are saved for the evenings when they have finished their work for the day. We do limit the time they have on it so that they retain some other interests.

Trevor advises caution when buying software:

We don't have much educational software on the computer as we think that a lot of it is designed for school use and is not really suitable for home. It's very difficult to assess whether or not software is really going to be useful and good value for money and it's possible to make some expensive mistakes. We do use CD-ROMs and the internet for finding information, though. We think the most important thing for the children at this stage is for them to be at home with the computer. Later on they will be able to learn about the different software packages which are in use in the business world.

Alison preferred to wait before getting a computer:

We have just got our first computer. The children are 11 and 9, and we didn't want to get one earlier as we think there's a danger that computers may take away other aspects of a child's creativity when they are very young. We would have spent far less time on reading, drawing, painting and imaginative things if the lure of the computer had been there in the earlier years!

Paul, an IT professional, has another view:

Computers are definitely here to stay and we would be failing our children if we didn't make sure that they had the right skills for the future. But things move on so rapidly that in ten years' time detailed knowledge of software and hardware gained today will probably be obsolete. It's our aim for our children's primary education to give them self-confidence and the courage to get stuck in and solve the problems. A good overall knowledge of computing is all that's necessary at this stage, plus creative thinking skills and expertise at problem-solving.

Computers have revolutionized the world of work. Home education offers an opportunity for children to learn essential IT skills at an early age if you wish. Once children become confident and interested in the possibilities they may go ahead to discover an astonishing amount about computing for themselves.

Art
Most young children enjoy art activities of all kinds and some may be passionate about them. The messy aspects of art and craft may be daunting to some families with children learning at home but it helps to be well prepared. Some families make room for an art corner somewhere in the house so that the materials don't need to be packed

away completely each time. A big plastic sheet for the floor may be useful, with another piece for the table. Some specialist fabric shops and department stores sell protective sheeting on a roll, or you could try a DIY store or a builder's merchant. It's worth getting a small easel or toy blackboard for suspending their paper on when they are painting as this is much more comfortable for them than working on a flat table. Spill-proof water pots are also well worth the investment!

There is a huge variety of different activities and you don't have to spend a fortune on the materials. Home-made playdough is cheap and endlessly fascinating for younger children. Saltdough modelling for older ones offers possibilities for detailed and sophisticated creations which may be baked, painted and varnished. Young children enjoy collecting natural materials for use in all sorts of artwork. Activities include junk modelling, collage, drawing, painting, cutting and sticking, wet paper painting, painting with sponges, printing with potatoes, cork or polystyrene, stencilling and a host of other possibilities. You should find some helpful books about art ideas in the junior section of the library.

If you have a scrap store nearby you can make savings on an exciting range of materials and trimmings, and some fabric and haberdashery stores have large selections of various beads, braids, glittery trimmings and sequins. Some families get together with friends to buy in bulk from educational suppliers, and in some areas it's possible for a group of families to buy educational supplies and art materials from the consortium that supplies the local schools and playgroups. To do this it's necessary for the group to have an informal committee and a 'clubs and societies' bank account which allows them to have a cheque book. Details may be obtained from the local education authority's county supplies department, but they are unable to deal with individual families. The group will have a big catalogue containing every conceivable kind of educational material so that they can buy in bulk. Very worthwhile savings may be made in this way.

How should parents at home go about developing children's artistic skills? Opinions vary. Practise using different media and introduce them to as many as you can. Encourage them to experiment. Some art educators say firmly that children should be left to express themselves. Others say they need guidance and ideas for making progress and learning techniques. Be wary of imposing adult perceptions on children's art and always respect the way they see things. Criticism of their work, however slight, may be fatal.

Help them to notice things as they are out and about, particularly concentrating on visual and spatial awareness as well as on colours and shapes and textures. Encourage children to experience the reality of things with all their senses instead of merely conveying information to them by means of words. Developing their perceptions will change and deepen the way they express themselves artistically. Visit art galleries and experience all kinds of art. Encourage them to respond to art by noticing how it makes them feel and also noticing what it conveys emotionally and non-verbally.

Rachel saw art as very important for her children:

> Our children enjoyed scribbling on anything when they were very young, especially the walls. Then as their coordination developed they made marks on the paper which stood for important items in their world – often Mummy and Daddy. These symbols are re-markably similar from child to child, even when a child hasn't seen the work of others. Over the years we watched our children repeat and refine their favourite images. Our children told stories through drawing pictures and talking, but they weren't keen on writing. They saw no need for it at this stage. We fostered this means of creative communication and we didn't force the writing issue. It's interesting that when they did get round to writing stories for themselves they both developed a rich vocabulary and interesting images, and I'm sure that the early non-verbal stories contributed a lot to this ability.

As children's perceptions change their symbolism becomes more complex and detailed. By age 9 or 10 most children become dissatisfied with their artistic efforts and they aim for greater realism through detail. They begin to outgrow their early childhood symbolic art and they become frustrated at their inability to draw things realistically. It is at this stage that they often announce that they hate drawing and give up altogether. Many adults are stuck at this stage, having never got beyond it themselves.

It helps to know that this experience is very common indeed and it is not a reflection of your lack of skill in teaching art! Learning the technique of drawing is only part of the answer. A really liberating book is Betty Edwards' *Drawing on the Right Side of the Brain* (1993).

Music

There are lots of possibilities for music at home and in the community. Even children who are in school receive most of their tuition from music teachers who are outside the school system.

Children respond to music from the earliest days and there are plenty of musical resources available on tape and CD as well as on radio and television. Most young children don't need much en-couragement to join in with their favourite songs, especially if there are actions to perform as well. Listening is very important too, and not only listening to music. Listen to the rhythms in nature, including the sea, raindrops, the music that streams make, the sounds of the wind and the sounds of birdsong. The simple activities of the pre-school years lead on naturally to more complex forms of music-making if you watch for opportunities.

Chris was uncertain at first:

> We thought that music might be a bit of a specialist area which could be difficult to do at home, but we were surprised at just how much is available out there. There are lots of concerts and recitals at our local community arts centre and many of the matinée performances are specially aimed at schools and young people. We found that we could get the schools' discount when we explained that we were home educating, and we have often benefited from booking as a group since we've been meeting up with other home educators. Recently we've been to an early music concert, a steel band event, a gamelan concert and an afternoon featuring youth choirs. It's good for the children to experience different kinds of music from other ages and cultures.

Barbara sees the advantages of home education for young musicians:

> The children have always enjoyed music and dance and we didn't want them to miss out on the kind of things they do at school. In fact, they are probably better off at home musically as friends with children at school tell us that there's not much time for music in an overcrowded school curriculum these days. Jenny is 6 and Matthew is 4. Jenny goes to an after-school music and dance class which is very popular and she has taken part in several informal performances. These are very good as the children then get used to performing to an audience, and Jenny loves to be on stage. Several other home educated children go as well.
>
> As well as the after-school class, we get together with other home educating families from time to time and one of our favourite activities is singing. Last month we had a very successful workshop where the children all made drums, rain-makers and a variety of shakers from junk materials, beans and so on. At home we don't have room for a piano but we have a reasonable electronic keyboard which both children will have the opportunity to learn to play.

June has learned something herself:

> I've finally got to grips with the difference between duple and

triple time and the difference between major and minor keys! I can remember being puzzled by these and other musical things when I was at school myself, and I just didn't manage to get the idea then. I took my daughter out of primary school last year and we do music along with the other subjects at home. I felt really worried about it at first but there are some very good, colourful and simple introductory books available for beginner musicians now. We have been working through a first piano book and the explanations are very good. My daughter is keen to continue with the piano so we are looking for a teacher for her. We are happy with this as we would have had to pay for lessons if she had been in school anyway.

As with all creative activities it's very important to nurture the child's interest and enthusiasm by offering as much variety as you can and by looking for opportunities that will provide inspiration and enjoyment. Specialist expertise within the home isn't necessary in order to give your child a good start in music.

If your child shows promise on a particular instrument, find the best teacher that you can and concentrate on fostering the child's creativity and imagination in other artistic areas as well. A holistic approach may help to reduce the risk of burnout, which is a particular problem for young performers.

These are the main areas to consider but this account is by no means definitive. In addition children at home may experience a whole range of interesting and useful practical activities including cooking, meal planning, caring for younger children, gardening, looking after animals, helping with the decorating and making things. There are opportunities for using tools and for learning about planning practical projects, costing and measuring. Outside the home, you may find that you can involve your children in social, environmental and community issues as well. There are also many other learning opportunities which parents may wish to explore with their children of primary age; your children's interests and enthusiasms may be a valuable guide. Many parents believe that an essential part of home education is to introduce their children to as many new experiences as possible, thus developing their ability to respond positively to new challenges.

CHAPTER 6

Projects

Learning through projects is an open-ended approach to education which is very popular at home with children and young people of all ages. This way of working is ideal for home as you are free from the constraints of the school timetable, and you can choose to spend as much time as you like on a project. One teenager whom we know spent at least a year working on a project about the Fire Service, and this topic broadened his knowledge right across the curriculum and led to some remarkable experiences for him. Our comments and ideas in this chapter are presented as a continuum from primary to secondary level as it's not helpful to draw an arbitrary line between them. The child's interest and general level of ability will determine where you start with a project and how far you go with it.

There is a limitless number of projects and topics that may be completed, and these may be as brief or as extended as you choose. Two examples are discussed in detail below to give you an idea of the possibilities. There are many ways of working on a project or topic, but some children need more guidance than others with the task of organizing the material. Projects may be simple or complex and the same topic may be explored at different levels. If you have children of different ages, they may enjoy working on the same project in different ways according to their ages and abilities.

An example of a simple project for young learners might perhaps be 'Birds in the Garden' (or in the park, or in the woods, or on the beach ...). You could suggest that you watch for birds together and identify them using a bird book. Then do some drawings of the birds, name them and find out some facts about them: what they eat, what their nests look like, what colour their eggs are, where they spend the winter and so on. One interesting observation about each bird may be enough for younger children as it's important to keep involvement by making sure that the work doesn't become burdensome.

Alternatively, he or she could think about their own reaction to each bird and write something descriptive about them. The project might consist of just a few pages which may be stored in a ring binder, and other topics might be added as you go along.

Slightly older children might like to look at birds in more depth. You could discuss the topic and identify a list of areas which might be of interest. Some of the following might emerge from your discussion: how many different birds can we identify in our area? Can we put them into groups? (birds of prey ... seed eaters ... insect eaters ... carrion birds, etc. ... different families of birds including tits, finches, warblers and so on). Why do birds migrate and where do they go? How are different birds adapted for the food they eat? A study of an interesting bird family, perhaps owls and their habits? A study of the birds of a particular area, for instance birds of the moorland, birds of the sea-shore, woodland birds, etc. ... colouring and camouflage ... male, female and juvenile plumage ... the structure of feathers and their properties and so on.

Young people of secondary age might take another approach. Discussion might yield some of the areas mentioned above, plus some of the following: How do birds fly? (wing shape, structure, feathers ...) A study of migration patterns. The evolution of birds from their pre-historic ancestors. The bird's digestive system. The structure of the egg. A study of birds who nest in unusual places. Birds and people, including: game birds and their management ... falconry ... carrier pigeons and pigeon racing ... doves and dovecotes ... turkeys (where did they come from?) ... threatened species. Birds in art (peacocks, owls, eagles, swans ...) and perhaps birds in mythology. And cooking with eggs for some practical work (nutritional content ... why we add them to cakes, etc. ... meringues ... their setting properties including egg custard and quiche ... other uses including glazing pastry and so on). Poems about birds and flying ... perhaps written in the form of a bird. Bird mobiles (one young person drew several dozen beautiful double-sided pictures of different birds, cut them out and hung them at different heights from a nylon thread which was suspended across the room) and collages. There are lots of opportunities for artwork, maps, photographs, drawings, creative work and research of different kinds including finding information on the internet.

Topic webs

Sometimes there are so many ideas and connections you could include that it's difficult to know where to begin. A topic web may provide a creative way of selecting material for a theme or a project. When you have decided on your topic, put the title in a circle in the centre of a piece of paper with lots of space around it.

This is how you might work on the topic of 'Communication'.

Decide on a definition: what is communication? This might be in the centre of your web.

Spend some time discussing, thinking and looking up connections. Collect all your ideas on a piece of paper, maybe over a couple of days. You may want to add some new ones and discard some that you decide not to follow up. Then organize the ideas into themes or subheadings around the central point. The topic web might look like the example in Figure 6.1, and it might form the first page of your project folder.

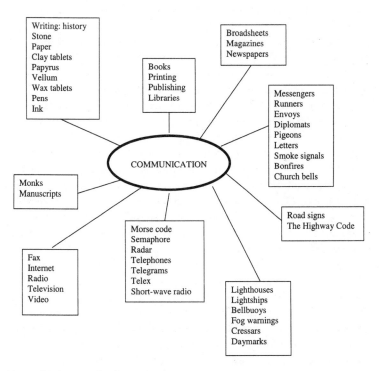

Figure 6.1 *An example of a topic web*

The subheadings may be worked on in any order and the responses may be as brief or as detailed as you wish. Encourage the young learners to ask questions about each aspect of the project and then to find the answers from their reading and research. Copying out large chunks of books is a pointless activity; they will get much more out of their fact-finding if they ask themselves: 'What do I want to find out about ... ?' and 'What is this chapter/section/article telling me about ... ?' Alternatively, you could discuss together and prepare a brief list of questions which would form the framework of a piece of writing about each heading. The answers to the questions could then be put together without numbers as a paragraph or more about each topic. You might use information from books plus information on CD-ROM, material from the internet, maps, drawings, pictures, photographs, brochures, guide books, postcards, sketches, diagrams, models, interviews, your own thoughts and observations, creative and imaginative writing and anything else you can find.

Remember that not everything has to be recorded; some aspects of the project may be a vivid and inspirational part of the learner's experience of the subject but there may be nothing visible to show for them.

Projects always come alive if you can incorporate any visits and trips into your studies. This will depend on where you live and, depending on the project, it may need some detective work. For the project described above, museums would be good places to start. Some cathedrals and churches have libraries with ancient manuscripts to see. You could also watch out for different road signs when you are out and talk about how they convey their message. Look at the Ordnance Survey map of your area and you may spot a 'Telegraph Hill' or a ' ... Beacon' or 'Beacon Hill' which you might visit as an excuse for a picnic. These are all places where signal beacons would have been sited in past times. Discover what you can see from the top ... take photographs ... imagine the chain of beacons lit in times of war or danger. If you are able to visit the coast you will find lots of examples of ways of communication there as well.

These examples show some of the ways in which you can make connections and put material together creatively in order to explore a theme and learn about it. A word of warning, though: not all children enjoy working in this way. Try not to be disappointed if your child loses interest despite your efforts to help, and be prepared to drop the project and move on to something else. Some learners do best with short, focused, definite tasks and they don't feel comfortable with the wide-ranging project approach.

When you are learning at home it's possible to experiment with different ways of working until you find the styles that suit your child best.

CHAPTER 7

Learning at home in the secondary years

Parents often worry about the transition from primary to secondary age. They are happy with helping their children to learn at the primary level but they fear that they will be out of their depth when it comes to the different subjects that make up the secondary school curriculum. Have courage! The distinction between primary and secondary education is an artificial one introduced by the school system. Experienced home educators will tell you that the education gradually becomes more complex and wide-ranging as their children's understanding develops and matures. So nothing changes overnight. A couple of new subjects are added at secondary level in school, but home educators may add or drop subjects or topics at any time as the national curriculum does not apply to them.

At Key Stage 3 of the national curriculum pupils at school study the same subjects as they did at Key Stage 2 together with a modern foreign language. From 2002 citizenship will become a compulsory subject as well at secondary level. A table of the Key Stages and their ages is given at the beginning of Chapter 5.

We must repeat here that the word 'curriculum' should not be taken to mean a formal, structured education. A curriculum may be a complete learning package, a set of educational plans or a descriptive outline of the general areas of knowledge which are covered during education at home.

Looking ahead
Some families are resolute in their commitment to informal or autonomous education during the secondary years, and it is their right to continue to educate in this way if they wish. Others like to look ahead and undertake some planning for the years to come. This may be a reassuring exercise too if you feel a bit daunted by the idea of home education at secondary level. Some investigation at this stage may help

to banish any anxieties about the future. There is no set time for doing this; some families like to know what is ahead of them when their children are still very young, while others are content to wait until they are around 12 or 13 years of age.

When you feel the need to look to the future you could look at some GCSE syllabuses – now known officially as 'subject specifications' – to discover what is involved in studying them. Take particular note of the syllabus aims which are separate from the subject content. Work backwards from this when considering how to proceed with your learner during the lower secondary years. There is a cluster of skills required for exam work which can be developed naturally in your work in the pre-GCSE years and these skills are used across the whole range of subjects.

Skills for learning

- good reading and understanding (comprehension skills)
- scanning and skimming texts to find information
- making good, clear diagrams
- analysing material including texts, pictures, facts, tables, graphs and lists
- memorizing information
- revision skills
- note-taking
- listening skills
- putting things in your own words
- concentrating and being focused
- finding information
- discussion
- general knowledge of everyday affairs and forming opinions
- presenting arguments
- drawing conclusions
- thinking logically and reasoning
- selecting and arranging material
- organizing your work and your time so that you can finish work in a set time
- and getting on with the work even if you'd rather be on the beach!

Many of these skills develop naturally through intelligent and worthwhile activities in daily life and learning. There is no evidence to suggest that learners are disadvantaged when they study for GCSE if they have not followed Key Stage 3 of the national curriculum. We have heard of many young students who have achieved good results at

GCSE after having studied quite informally in the lower secondary years. The subject content of different GCSE courses is self-contained and starts from basics, and you'll find more information about these and other examinations in Chapter 10.

Subjects and topics

For some young people the best way of organizing home education is to concentrate on English, maths and a series of topics which may have a bias towards the creative or the practical, or projects which are based on hobbies or interests. Chapter 6 outlines ways of doing project work which apply to children and young people of all ages. Use of a computer and spellchecker may help by making writing less of a chore.

Others prefer to move to a subject-based approach when their learners are approaching secondary age. These are the normal school subjects, but home educators are not obliged to study them all: English, maths, science, modern foreign languages, history, geography, religious education, ICT, design and technology, art, music and physical education – and citizenship from 2002.

If you decide to study some or all of the above as separate subjects you might like to refer to some of the study guides which are available in most bookshops for Key Stage 3 and GCSE level. These are not complete courses but some parents use them as a starting-point. There are study guides for every subject and you could use the contents as a basis for making your own list of topics to cover.

There are many other subjects that you can learn about, most of which will lead to a qualification if desired. These are just some of them: agriculture, botany, geology, astronomy, childcare and child development, British Sign Language, car and motorcycle maintenance, philosophy, law, social studies, archaeology, drama and theatre studies, pottery, photography, business studies, electronics, Latin, Greek and a host of other ancient or modern languages, food and nutrition, horticulture – and home educated teenagers have also been known to study conjuring and circus skills!

Materials and resources for learning

There are a few basic items which you'll need right from the beginning but most things are optional. Apart from the obvious requirement for the usual stationery and ring binders, you'll need a calculator for maths and other subjects. When you buy it, make sure that it's on sale as suitable for GCSE so that you won't have to replace it later. A good dictionary and an atlas are important reference tools, and it's useful to have a children's encyclopaedia on the shelf as well. These are also available on CD-ROM or on the internet if you have a computer, but computers aren't essential. They may be very useful but some families manage perfectly well without them. You don't need correspondence courses either, and if you have started home education recently it's always best to wait until you've settled in to it before making any expensive purchases.

If you have just taken your children out of school, you will need to find out their capabilities before you can get suitable books and resources. Looking at any work that was done at school recently will help, but it may take a while for gaps in the young person's knowledge to become apparent. Once you have a rough idea of what areas you are going to cover it's worth visiting a bookshop to see what's available. Allow plenty of time for examining the books very critically. Are the books readable, well presented and clearly laid out? Are the tasks in them worth doing and are they possible at home? If they aren't suitable for home use, can you see ways of adapting the material?

Some parents scour charity shops for second-hand books. Even if they are outdated in some respects you may find that they have useful ideas in them which may be adapted and brought up to date. The illustrations and text may look comical and old-fashioned but you may be able to adapt and use ideas, questions and activities from them to make materials that are relevant to your child.

Some young people like to have worksheets and quizzes to help them to focus on a subject, and illustrations may make them appealing especially if your child is a visual learner. Whether you are designing your own activity sheets and questions or using materials from a book, think carefully about what the child will learn from doing the activity. Is it worthwhile?

Choosing your areas of interest

It's very important for young people at home to feel fully involved in decisions about what they learn and how they go about it. Many young people will have developed distinct learning preferences by this stage. At home not all work needs to be finished. If your child starts something and loses interest, don't be afraid to abandon it and try something else.

Our experience suggests that older children who learn at home tend to specialize far more than their peers at school. Often an interest develops and the learner gives it much more time than would be possible at school. Clearly this is a factor in success later. There is no particular reason why a home education curriculum should be 'broad' or 'balanced' as the law requires of the school curriculum. Breadth and balance may easily lead to mediocrity if young people have no chance to spend time on the areas of knowledge about which they are passionately enthusiastic. When there's a strong commitment to a particular subject it's usually necessary to move outside of mainstream education in order to pursue it. For example, we know of a specialist music school somewhere in Russia where the young musicians spend eight hours a day sleeping, eight hours a day living, learning, eating and relaxing, and eight hours a day involved with their music. It's easy to see that their curriculum couldn't be described as 'balanced', but they are committed to the choice that they have made and their musical achievements are exceptional.

So don't feel obliged to give equal attention to all the subjects below; your child may find that some areas are of much more interest than others. Some of these may be ignored altogether and that's perfectly reasonable. Some of the subject areas which are outlined below begin with ideas for young people who aren't particularly interested in studying the subject in depth. We have then moved on to include information of a more specialist nature, but we urge you not to feel intimidated by these details if your child prefers to adopt a low-key approach to the subject!

You may worry about a child pursuing an interest only to find that the interest changes later. This does happen but it's vital to remember that the knowledge and experience gained during the period of enthusiasm is never wasted. Exams or vocational qualifications may be added later on, and some people get through them with great speed once they discover that certain qualifications are necessary for their future plans.

Learning at home in the secondary years

The curriculum notes which follow at this point are not given as a recommended method for home education. They are not intended to be prescriptive. We have not attempted to provide a complete curriculum in all subjects for children of all ages. Further, these notes are not intended to be a guide to the national curriculum although some reference is made to school subjects. There are no boundaries to learning at home and there are many different ways of teaching and learning. The ideas below are intended to help parents who don't know where to start, and they may serve as a guide for families as they approach the secondary years at home. Each section ends with some reference to GCSE, but there is more information on examinations in Chapter 10.

English

At the beginning of the secondary stage young people's literacy skills may be at widely differing stages of development. Some will be working hard on basic English especially if there have been problems in school. There may be a degree of dyslexia or other learning problem. Some will lack confidence and they may be very reluctant to write anything, especially if they are active young people who learn best when all their senses are engaged on a task. Writing may be a laborious activity that is not enjoyed. Some may dislike writing although they are good at it. Others will be producing competent English and they will be ready for more demanding work. Some will be writing effortlessly and turning out well-crafted, thoughtful and mature prose. All these learners will need different tasks and individual approaches to reading and to written work. Young people all have different strengths and it is reasonable to expect them to have reached varying levels of achievement in writing by the time they reach 16.

Reading widely enriches a young person's vocabulary and prose style and it also improves spelling in most cases. If reading is not yet a fluent and comfortable process the young person may have problems with written work even if there are no specific learning difficulties. There are also lots of instances where children may read well but their skills in written work are not very well developed. You may find that you need to work with your child on the basic elements of writing sentences and paragraphs. Some children may also need help in order to learn how to plan their written work. Some parents become actively involved with their children's writing, adopting an 'apprenticeship' approach to learning. Skills that are developed through English are fundamental to other subjects, so it is reasonable to spend extra time on basic literacy if necessary even if it means restricting the time which is given to other areas of the curriculum.

Angela's experience offers some useful tips:

Richard came out of school during the last year of primary school. He had missed a lot of school and he was very unhappy. He believed he was a failure and he thought he was no good at anything. We had quite a long break from formal work until he agreed that he was ready to give it a try again. He knew that we would have to work on reading, writing and maths most of all at first and we went right back to things that he did years ago.

Most of the workbooks that were available for English were based on materials to reinforce work done at school during the literacy hour, and we found that all the technical terms and the general approach were no good at all for him. I use passages out of a children's encyclopaedia about topics which interest him and I make up questions for him to answer. We read the passage together and he goes away and writes down the answers. This does help him to read carefully for understanding and he also learns about lots of different topics while he's doing it.

He likes writing tasks which are quite short, otherwise he gets overwhelmed and this makes him angry. Another thing we do is to choose some simple items – a marble, a teapot, an owl, a banana, a bonfire, the moon, among others – and write five sentences about each one. He does wonderful illustrations to go with them and he's getting quite proud of his collection. It might not look much to an outside observer, but I know just how far he's come since he started learning at home.

Reading

Some 11-year-olds will be reading titles from the *Banana Books* series and others will be on to *Jane Eyre* or *The Lord of the Rings*. It is not possible to say which books they should be reading as abilities vary so greatly, and it makes sense to start from where they are rather than from a list of recommended books.

Sometimes it may be hard to maintain the young learner's interest in reading at this stage. This may be because reading is hard work for the child, and in this case constant encouragement and support will be needed. Many children have difficulty finding books that they like in the library. Learning to make a quick assessment of a book by glancing at it, studying the cover and reading a few extracts is a skill that you can teach them, and you can also help by making sure that they are familiar with the way the library works. Library staff are usually pleased to help young readers to find out more about the library especially if you ask at a quiet time.

Try poetry, short stories, non-fiction texts, selections from newspapers, magazines and material that is related to the young person's interests. Some young people still enjoy being read to well into the teenage years and this may help to keep them interested in books. And it's good to do some yourself to encourage a culture of reading. Adults can help by keeping in touch with the young reader's interests and skill at reading so that they can suggest suitable titles, and you may find that you revisit some old favourites and discover some new ones. If books have always been part of family life and other members of the family enjoy reading, it is more likely that young people will become keen readers who are aware of the pleasures that books have to offer.

Well-established young readers will be constantly on the lookout for new experiences in reading, including literature from before the twentieth century.

Writing

When children have a good command of written English you can move on by presenting them with as many different types of writing as possible, reading and discussing a range of texts and encouraging them to create examples of their own. Encourage them to notice how to adapt the style and vocabulary of the writing to suit the occasion and the audience. Some young people need quite a lot of help with this while others seem to have an instinctive awareness of appropriate language. Among other types you can look at factual writing, letters both formal and informal, diaries, making notes and summaries, writing to express opinions and arguments, persuasive and powerful writing, humour and satire, reports, biographical and autobiographical work, imaginative writing and poetry.

Some English course materials have passages with questions to test understanding and these exercises do help to deepen the young person's response to the written word. There is also a lot of interesting and useful work to be done by looking at writing in the media, especially the expression of fact, opinion and bias, sensational and emotional writing, logical writing, comment and the importance of presentation. These aspects of language are relevant in very many areas of life and learning.

Imaginative writing may be started off in various ways. Some young writers will seize enthusiastically upon a title or on an opening sentence, or on the merest hint of a situation which immediately unfolds itself to them. Others need more stimulus to get the ideas flowing. Sometimes it helps to discuss their ideas and brainstorm the possibilities. There are some good starting-points which may be based on characters in favourite books, films or television programmes, including imaginary adventures and perhaps diaries or letters written by them. Much creative writing may arise from the young person's own experience. Your knowledge of your child's own opinions and preoccupations may be useful when you are looking for topics and ideas that will appeal. Some young people may produce interesting and thoughtful writing after considering a picture or some expressive music. Even actual items which are real and perhaps unfamiliar – Granny's brooch, an old photograph, an unusual stone or natural object and so on – may spark off a story, a poem or a piece of descriptive writing.

Some young people enjoy creative writing but others find it difficult. It's good to encourage and bring out the ability which is there but try not to be concerned if your child really doesn't want to be creative in this way.

When you are helping young people to develop and improve their written work it's very important to be aware of the level of skill that they have reached. It's all too easy to fall into the trap of imposing adult perceptions and imagination on a child's creativity. The creative aspect of writing needs a sensitive response as it is a subjective process. How can you best help a child who is 'stuck'? It's very tempting for willing adults to rush in and tell their young writers how their story should end or finish that poem for them. Perhaps it's more helpful if you ask your child to explain the problem, listen creatively and discuss the options without actually taking over the task. Often the act of explaining is enough to enable the young writer to see ways round the difficulty. Asking questions around the situations may also be helpful in getting the inspiration going again.

No two people will create the same piece of writing from the same stimulus, and making judgements about another person's creativity is a difficult and potentially dangerous matter. We may make constructive criticisms about technical points of grammar, logic and spelling but when it comes to the subject of the writing itself, who are we to say that our ideas and approaches are better? It's possible to suggest other approaches which might have been chosen and you could discuss other ways of planning the writing and selecting the details, but it would be right to offer these as options and not as improvements. Young people need positive encouragement and support to help them develop confidence in their own creative powers.

Too many suggestions for improvement may be demoralizing and hurtful especially if the young person has worked hard to produce a piece of writing. It's important always to respond positively and respectfully to the piece as a whole before discussing details of grammar or spelling. Choose a few points and comment on them, perhaps encouraging the learner to write them out at the end of the work. Spelling may be improved by learning some words which come up regularly and some young people like to keep a notebook with problem words in. It's often easier to remember how to spell a word if you include it in a short (preferably amusing) sentence or phrase. Some young people are very resistant to planning written work and many don't like re-drafting their work, although these are standard fare according to the national curriculum. It's not a good idea to insist on these things as young learners often come to see for themselves eventually that these aspects of writing may actually be helpful.

Speaking and listening

Speaking and listening are skills in English which usually develop very naturally and easily at home. Indeed, home educators have a definite advantage in respect of these areas as they have so many opportunities for conversation and discussion of ideas and opinions. Teachers in school need to plan activities to encourage speaking and listening but for home educators they are a natural part of daily life. Finally, it might also be worth mentioning that drama is a popular choice of leisure activity among home educated young people; fortunately, drama classes and groups are widespread everywhere.

Maths

As with science, many parents have worries about maths at home when their children come to the end of the primary years. Parents often say that they can't do maths and they are frightened at the prospect of being responsible for their children's maths education. Sadly, this is a comment on the kind of maths that was taught in the past which has robbed people of their confidence in the subject. It's reassuring to note that there have been big changes in maths in recent years.

The great thing is to remain calm. When they are faced with a problem that their child can't understand, most people find that they can work it out if they look methodically at it and follow the worked examples in the textbook. Sometimes it helps to look up the answer and work backwards from it to see how to get there. This is not cheating!

By the start of young people's secondary education there is a wide range of abilities and rates of progress. There is also a considerable range of expectations; some children may be tackling GCSE maths at 11 years or younger while others are concentrating on basic survival skills until the end of their secondary education. The main thing is to help learners to enjoy maths, to be confident and to achieve as much as they can. It's crucial to set realistic goals in maths for your child.

First find out what they need to do next. This is relatively easy if you have been educating at home for some time as you will know what they have covered. If you are just starting out it will help to look at their work from school and discuss it with them. It's very important to make sure that they have understood the foundations of maths, as research has shown that many children have problems with secondary maths because they haven't mastered the basics at primary level. You may find that you have to go back a stage and work through a range of topics with them in order to consolidate their knowledge. Home Education Advisory Service offers the *HEAS Maths Pack* (2000) for use at Key Stage 3, and it contains useful assessment materials to help parents to find out where their children are in maths.

Most large bookshops will have a range of different books and maths schemes. Revision guides have their uses but they are very concentrated and they do assume that the material has already been covered. To start with you may want to work your way through a course or textbook together. All the courses and textbooks will cover the same topics as it is impossible to buy any which are published in the UK these days which are not lined up with the national curriculum. Layout (are the pages crowded?), language (is it suitable for your child's ability in reading?), colour (is it appealing and attractive?), level (is it aiming towards a particular level at GCSE later on?), help (does it have a teacher's book or answers?) and general presentation and clarity are all things to be considered before buying maths materials. If you are unsure, have a longer look at the book very carefully at home. If the book is unused, most bookshops will agree to an exchange or a refund if they hold the item in stock normally.

Computer software for maths may be entertaining but it's not essential, and it's no substitute for a good textbook. It's difficult to assess its value unless you know someone who is using it already.

You will have noticed that maths materials at primary level contain a lot of practical work. This is in keeping with current thinking in maths teaching that emphasizes learning maths skills by doing. This approach in the early years leads on naturally to investigations in maths. The concept of mathematical investigations may be new to you if you didn't have to do them when you were at school. Briefly, investigations are extended, open-ended tasks and problems which don't have a predetermined method for solving them. Work in investigations means finding out the method at the same time by looking for patterns, testing theories, seeing logical connections and analysing information. There may not be any 'right' answers and the work may be completely original. An investigation may take a long time to do and you may have to keep on coming back to it to try a new line of enquiry or to test your theories.

It's useful for learners to do some investigative work and it may be a liberating experience for children who are intimidated by fears of getting the answers wrong. Investigations promote creativity and logical thought and most adults are familiar with the principles involved although they may not realize it. Maths textbooks all contain investigations now as they are an established part of the school curriculum. The skills learned in doing investigations are helpful later on in coursework for GCSE.

Even if you feel very unsure about maths, don't assume that you'll need a tutor. Give it a try first as parent and learner and you may be able to find the way forward together. The young person may be able to work alone with occasional input from you. Children may need to gain confidence in their own reasoning powers first if they have come out of school and are used to the presence of a teacher.

Sometimes a child comes out of school with a problem. Marguerite's son Danny was in despair while he was in school, but he is making progress:

> We're slowly getting there. He got a mental block about maths when he was at school. He always seemed to be last to finish and he says that he couldn't concentrate in the lessons. I think he just gave up in the end. He's 13 now and we have been going over all the primary stuff – arithmetic, decimals, fractions, measuring length and area, mass and capacity, problems involving money and some basic work on circles and triangles. I realized recently that he had forgotten how to tell the time on an ordinary clockface as he sees digital clocks and watches so much. He's trying really hard and he does have a problem with forgetting things. We have to keep on coming back to basics again so we're not covering very much new material, but we'll be happy if he can be competent in the maths that he'll need for living by the time he reaches 16.
>
> When we started home education we made a list of the areas of maths that we hoped to cover with Danny. We did this by going through the chapters in a maths textbook to choose from the topics that were in it. First there was the really essential maths and then there was a list of other topics for interest which we hoped to introduce as well. We make notes, use colours, put examples on the wall, say tables all the time and do lots of practical things to help it to stick. He finally got the idea of 'borrowing' after sitting down with piles of coins and counting out pennies and ten pence pieces to give change. I try to approach maths with him through woodwork and other practical projects, so our maths is part of everyday life. We use several different books for variety.

Tracey explains her family's commitment to informal learning in maths:

> Our children have never been to school and we have always educated them informally without any plans or structures. The children aren't forced to learn and we see no reason to change just because they are teenagers. They decide what they want to learn and we trust them to know what they need. They have learned maths as they needed it. Ever since the early days basic arithmetic just happened by doing things. Ryan soon learned about money and counting his change, and Ash has made his aviary and bought the birds. They've found out all sorts of

mathematical knowledge from cooking and gardening and building projects.

There are maths books around if they want to use them. There are probably gaps in their knowledge but we think it's more important for them to be learning what they want to learn. And we know a home educating family in London with a daughter who had done absolutely no formal study of maths before starting a GCSE maths course at age 14. She passed her exam a year later with a C grade. If they want to do exams later we'll support them, but it will be their decision.

Geeta's concern about maths at home is shared by many new home educators, but she says:

I was a bit bothered about the idea of doing maths with the children when they reached secondary school age, but I needn't have worried. It's actually been fine so far. We carried on with the books we had been using until our eldest daughter was 12, then we thought she was ready for the next stage. We looked at lots of maths courses before we committed ourselves and it was worth taking some trouble over choosing the right one. Our maths course should keep us going until the time for starting GCSE work and the younger children will follow on with it eventually. We found it quite easy to make a rough plan for the work by dividing the number of topics by the number of weeks that we would be working in two years, allowing some time in hand for unexpected things, some topics taking longer and so on.

Most of the time she works on her own and then comes and asks me if she doesn't understand and we look at it together. I'm not a lot of help, though! Still, if we do get stuck we can always ask my nephew who is good at maths. My daughter doesn't mind maths but it's not her favourite subject, and it doesn't come particularly easily to her. In spite of this she's getting ahead of herself and if she carries on at this rate she'll finish the course before we thought she would. So far there haven't been any big snags and everything is well explained with clear examples to follow.

Finally, a word about GCSE in maths. The subject specifications start from first principles. Although Key Stage 3 of the national curriculum leads in the direction of Key Stage 4 (GCSE level) it is not essential to follow Key Stage 3 work closely to be successful at GCSE. Thorough preparation of GCSE work is necessary for success but there is the freedom to explore different things beforehand without affecting the outcome at GCSE.

Science

The study of science is often perceived as a problem especially at secondary level and parents sometimes think that experimental and practical work is not possible at home. Not so. Families are often surprised to discover all the possibilities which are open to them, but although practical science is desirable and necessary it's more important to understand the processes involved. The history of science is another area of knowledge which is readily accessible to home educators and the stories of major scientific discoveries may be inspiring and exciting to young people.

And is the study of science relevant to young people generally? It's certainly not just a subject for the select few who want to become scientists. Some understanding of basic science is useful as we are increasingly surrounded by complex scientific equipment in our daily lives; having some idea of how things work is a great aid to using these things with safety and confidence. Also, scientific understanding helps young people to become well-informed adults as there are many major issues including genetic modification, cloning and environmental problems which cannot be understood without some scientific knowledge.

At home there is much to investigate in everyday objects including television, radio, mobile phones and telecommunications, electrical appliances and laser technology. Science at home allows for spontaneity in investigations which fosters the spirit of discovery. You do not need a laboratory in order to develop scientific ways of thinking. Young people may investigate the areas of science which interest them and acquire confidence in their ability to investigate, reason and find things out. Designing the experiment and improvising the equipment are part and parcel of the development of scientific ways of thinking and far more of a challenge than constructing a pre-arranged experiment which has been planned by the teacher at school.

Families' experiences of science at home are very varied. Leigh recalls:

My daughter studied chemistry to A level and she used a good-sized chemistry set available from toyshops throughout her studies. The equipment was small and it needed careful handling, but everything worked well. It was perfectly all right for what she wanted to do and it was useful all the way through.

Audrey explains her approach:

We carried on doing science pretty informally until Michael was 14. Then we looked at the topics in a science textbook and ticked off the ones we had investigated and we found that we had covered nearly everything in it anyway. So much arises in daily life and most children want to know how things work and why things happen.

Deborah's daughter Margaret (12 years) was bullied at school and she became school phobic and lost her self-confidence. Deborah says:

Margaret's work suffered as a result and she has a lot of ground to catch up on with her reading and basic maths. We give more time than most of our friends to work on maths and English. Science national curriculum-style would be a problem for us and she finds the language of textbooks very difficult. We don't study it separately as a subject but we read lots of interesting extracts from a junior science encyclopaedia, and I usually write out some questions for her to answer to help her to understand and remember. She is learning some science along the way and her reading is getting better. We do some simple practical work too but we don't push it as she really isn't very interested in science at the moment.

Before becoming a home educator, Sharon used to teach secondary science at school:

We found that it was possible to do plenty of practical work in physics, biology and chemistry at home. We collected up our science kit from around the kitchen, the garage and the toolbox and we had a big box for jam jars, yogurt pots, string, cork, bits of wood and wire, electrical bits and pieces and other useful things. Our 'lab' was a table in the garden shed. We bought a student microscope, a thermometer, some glassware and measuring equipment from an educational supplies catalogue and we found that we could manage to get hold of most chemicals. We bought a few things from a chemical supplier who accepted orders from us when they were accompanied by a letter from HEAS confirming that we subscribed to them. We did less practical work as they got older as it was time-consuming, and as exams approached we concentrated more on the processes and less on the practical side.

In my view the main purpose of practical work in the sciences at this level is to get students used to techniques of investigation and scientific enquiry and to help them to discover that science is exciting. Science at home is a totally different experience from school science and it needs a different approach. Investigating at home has a spontaneity and a spirit of adventure that is unique – it's not about merely replicating the experiments and obtaining the 'right' results. Our children were very interested to hear how

Cockerell discovered the principle of the hovercraft using a vacuum cleaner, empty tins and kitchen scales and they felt a certain kinship with him as they saw themselves as scientific adventurers too!

Bernard remembers:

The children were very interested in animals and plants when they were primary age and as they moved on they found biology the most interesting of the sciences. We studied biology with the help of the gerbils and our cat which obligingly produced several litters of kittens. We made a pond in the garden and that was an ongoing experiment in itself. We did a weather project which linked in with life in the pond and they learned an incredible amount about water plants, fish and insects. That led on to ecology and they got involved with the work of a local nature reserve. We found that everything joined together naturally and we didn't really plan it ... one thing just led on to another.

Science at home can mean many different things as parents make use of the resources that are available to them. Your work can also be suited to the child's needs, interests and abilities and you may give it as little or as much time as you think is appropriate.

As a postscript to the subject of science at home, it's interesting to note that for some time leading scientists have expressed reservations about the state of practical science teaching in schools. A study carried out by researchers at the Centre for Policy Studies in Education at the University of Leeds in 1999 called for the science curriculum to be reconsidered as it was too prescriptive and lacking in spontaneity, thereby taking the excitement out of science. In January 2001 Lord Winston, the chairman of the House of Lords' Science and Technology Committee, expressed his concern that experiments are being abandoned in schools because teachers fear legal action in the event of an accident. Evidence presented to the committee by distinguished scientists showed that pupils are reduced to watching teachers doing experiments as schools become further surrounded by health and safety regulations and stringent rules regarding disposal of chemicals.

Thus far home scientists are free of such restrictions and they rely on common sense and reasonable precautions to ensure that their children are safe from harm. We wonder if perhaps we are reaching the point where there's no place like home for budding scientists!

Young people may study physics, chemistry and biology at home and they may choose to take GCSE in the separate sciences or as combined science. Home educators are also able to investigate other sciences such as geology, astronomy, psychology or botany if they wish. Some families enjoy the challenge of doing coursework investigations at home and it's perfectly feasible to do this, but it's not essential. The International GCSE (IGCSE) offers combined and single award science options which have 'alternative to practical' papers which may be taken instead of coursework. These papers test the candidates' skills of analysis, observation and deduction in just the same way as a practical test. You can also choose to take a practical test at the examination centre instead of coursework if you wish, as long as the centre is willing to accommodate this option.

Languages

At home families have considerable choice when it comes to learning languages. It isn't obligatory to study another language at all if your child isn't interested, and it would make sense to delay or abandon foreign language study if there were major problems with basic English skills.

If you are starting language learning for the first time there are some points to consider when deciding which language to choose. Will your child be learning purely for general interest, to communicate with family or friends abroad or for a potential exam subject later on? If you're looking ahead to GCSE it would be a good idea to make sure that the language is offered by one of the examining bodies if your choice is one which is not generally taught in schools. If exam success later is important you may also like to consider how easy it will be to get materials and resources to help.

You don't need to be a language specialist to help your child to learn at home. There's a lot you can do especially in the early stages of learning a language. You could start by looking at several languages and you should find language courses available in your library. Larger libraries usually have a good choice of materials for a wide range of languages, providing a low-cost way of exploring the different options. Some television networks have foreign language channels which would be an excellent resource for learning.

There are many audio and multimedia courses available to buy, but there are some pitfalls. Young people may complain that some courses contain too much material about adult concerns such as employment and married life. If this is a problem try to find resources that are published for schools; these will have lots of information about school but if learners are preparing for GCSE they will need this anyway. Life at school is a staple topic in exams as the examiners believe that everyone will have experienced it and will have something to say about it. Some resources are meant to be used as revision aids and they are not intended to be used on their own as a course, so check carefully before you buy.

A native speaker of the chosen language may be able to give you a lot of help regardless of whether or not he or she has had teaching experience. Someone who is fluent in the language would be able to help the learner as and when necessary during the course and there is plenty of information available from the examining bodies to give guidance about the nature of the exam and the standards expected. There are several well-established correspondence courses available as well if you feel that your learner needs this level of help to make progress.

Some home educating families manage to arrange exchange visits, but a family holiday may be just as beneficial especially for a younger child.

If you are able to visit the country this would be a great help for pronunciation and for interest and enthusiasm. It would be a good opportunity to collect materials and information as well, including newspapers, magazines, children's periodicals, children's books, tapes and videos. Some young people who are familiar with Bible stories enjoy reading them in another language, so if this applies to your family it would be a good idea to bring a children's Bible back from your visit. If you can bring back some single copies of magazines it's usually possible to take out an overseas subscription by post using a credit card once you have the subscription details. Material for younger native speakers is ideal as the language is at about the right level of difficulty for young people working towards GCSE.

Working in this way you can still make good progress in another language even if there aren't regular opportunities to speak it. It may also be possible to enrol at a further education college for a part-time exam course, especially if you are willing to pay. Otherwise the young person could work alone to achieve a good grounding in the language and apply for a place at college, post-16. Susan explains how she studied for GCSE at home:

> I wanted to do French as I had learned it with a French family for several years when I was younger and I liked the language. I had another French friend who gave me some help for a while before the exam. I got quite good at the language itself but I realized when the exam was a few months away that I wasn't so good at speaking and listening. So I got as many French videos as I could and watched them over and over again. I borrowed all the ones in the library and in the video shop and my friend lent me some that she had for her children.

It was amazing because when I watched a video for the first time it was scary as I couldn't make any sense of it at all. Yet each time I watched it I understood a bit more. Some of them had subtitles and I covered them up with a strip of paper and only looked if I was really stuck. It was like magic as I found that after a while I could really hear what they were saying and the words gradually made sense in my head. I worked intensively at it but it was very satisfying and I got a grade A in my IGCSE exam.

If you're aiming at exams, get subject specifications and details well in advance to see what you are preparing for. Past papers and taped listening material are very helpful. Some examining groups provide lists of required vocabulary and grammar. Most examining groups have a speaking test which may involve role-playing, prepared conversation or a talk which is prepared beforehand. There is sometimes a passage for translation which might be prepared in advance on some papers, some comprehension tests and some written work in the language. GCSE papers will have coursework but IGCSE language papers have non-coursework options as well.

History

Some children love history while others are completely untouched by it. Fortunately, there are lots of different ways of discovering the past and families at home can choose from the entire range and scope of world history.

Even at secondary level some young people learn history almost without noticing it by visiting museums and exhibitions, taking part in history days and trips further afield, experiencing historical reenactments, visiting archaeological digs and looking at industrial history. Films, drama, videos and historical novels may all provide useful material and if you haven't already covered it you could consider looking into some family history. For some families history means a chronological study with timelines and dates but it's by no means essential to work in this way. It's a perfectly valid approach to explore a varied and unconnected series of historical subjects. As long as the young person's interest and enthusiasm is maintained, topics selected at random may be interrelated and linked together eventually.

Depending on where you live, local history may be of interest. Young people will probably notice some changes that have taken place in their own lifetime which they can record, then look back further. The library's local studies collection is likely to have some detailed and interesting materials including maps, records, photographs and written accounts of the history of the locality. Churchyards and churches are often good places to look as well.

One family prepared a history trail for some home educating friends. One of the young people writes:

> Our town has an old part which is very interesting and special. We decided to get some books from the library and find out about it so we could make a history trail. First we found a map of the area as it was about a hundred years ago. It was so detailed that you could even see what shops were there in those days. We made a list of all the interesting things that we could find out from the books, then we went to the area and looked for them. We found wonderful things from the past which were still there today including an old sundial, some amazing insurance marks, some windows that were painted on the walls and not real (we'd never noticed them before!), a very old postbox in a wall and some stocks in the churchyard.
>
> The best find was an old butcher's shop that had been turned into a house, but above the front window you could still see the big thick beam with the old hooks in where the butcher used to hang his meat. There must have been loads of flies! We made a map, a sheet of clues, facts and quiz questions for our friends so they could follow the trail and find all the hidden things that were so interesting. We loved making the trail as it made us look at the town in a new way, and it was good to share it with our friends.

History projects don't have to involve masses of writing. Photographs, audiotapes, videos, drawings, maps, making models, making plays and making quizzes are some of the other possible ways of recording your findings. Sometimes a different angle on writing may be interesting, and imaginative young people may enjoy writing as if they were a historical character. If this appeals there are lots of different creative possibilities including diaries, letters, poems, documents and so on.

Politics is a related subject which may become a passionate interest for some home educated young people, and this may lead to greater understanding of political history. Acquiring some knowledge of contemporary politics is not difficult with vast amounts of information available via television, newspapers and the internet. If young people can see how politics relates to them the subject becomes more interesting, so it's worth looking at local politics and local issues too.

A visit to Parliament may be worth investigating. Any UK resident may telephone their MP's secretary to arrange a visit, but you need to apply well in advance. Tours take place when the House is not sitting, usually Monday and Tuesday mornings and Friday afternoons. Your

MP might show you round in person and this would be a good time to raise the subject of home education! You will see the Central Lobby with its ornate mosaic ceiling, the Commons Chamber which is surprisingly small with its tiered rows of green seats, and the impressive House of Lords with the Monarch's throne and the Woolsack. It's also possible to watch a debate from the Strangers' Gallery. There may be a long queue for the Gallery and if you prefer you could apply to your MP for tickets, but apply well in advance as each MPs' allocation of tickets is limited.

What can you do if young people find history a complete non-event? Sometimes it's possible to find a way in through a particular topic or interest, fashion, for instance, or trains, scientific discoveries, motoring, a particular sport, medicine, education and so on. If nothing appeals to them they may just not be interested at the moment. In that case it's better to leave it and explore something else. Studying history is not obligatory and if they are not put off they are much more likely to come to it later on.

At school there is much emphasis on the skills needed in history and these skills may be encouraged readily at home without specialist input. Many of the skills developed in English studies are useful in history including good close reading and understanding, comprehension, analysis and the ability to summarize information. The ability to consider information critically helps the young person to detect bias in historical evidence. The evidence may be in the form of cartoons, pictures, speeches, diaries and so on. Young people need to be able to recognize and compare different forms of evidence and assess their reliability, and this requires the general skill of logical thinking and the ability to make observations and to deduce information from them. The examination of source materials includes distinguishing between primary sources (information which comes directly from someone who witnessed an event: including letters, photographs, documents and similar) and secondary sources ('hearsay' accounts or analyses written by people who were not eyewitnesses).

History textbooks published now are much more colourful and accessible than were some of the tomes which parents would have struggled through in their schooldays. Books which are designed for use at Key Stage 3 and Key Stage 4 all have exercises and assignments which are designed to develop the skills that are expected of young historians. These are usually given at the end of each chapter or section, and they may make a good framework for independent study for older ones.

Some parents are concerned about the risk that if they are 'marking' the work, they might not notice if the young person didn't get the emphasis right or didn't see all the implications of a question. Don't worry. Read the chapter carefully, consider the question for yourself and discuss it with the learner. Gather up as many points as you can and talk about the question together. It's useful to have more than one textbook to compare information and explanations.

GCSE History is a popular subject with private candidates. The emphasis at GCSE is on nineteenth- and twentieth-century history and world history of this time, but study of any period that is undertaken before beginning GCSE work will be beneficial.

Geography

Geography is a very wide-ranging subject. It includes the study of people and places all over the world; investigations into the way people and human activity have an impact on the environment; shopping, settlement, tourism, transport, agriculture, industry and other patterns of economic activity; disasters such as flooding, forest fires, landslides, avalanches and their causes and consequences; issues of pollution, sustainable development, conservation; the study of climate and weather patterns; investigation of different physical features including earthquakes, volcanoes, the structure of the earth's crust, rivers, lakes, coastlines, mountains, weathering, erosion; studies and comparisons of different countries and environments including rainforests, deserts, the polar regions and so on.

Many of the skills which are used in geography are also developed in other subjects. These include collecting and recording evidence and data in practical work and fieldwork, analysing it and drawing conclusions, drawing plans, maps, diagrams and graphs, using spreadsheets, word processing and databases on the computer and using maps, globes and atlases. As always, logical thinking and reasoning are essential.

There are many ways into the subject even if you haven't studied much geography before this stage. Projects may be short or long and may involve anything which inspires an interest in other parts of the world. There is a lot of fun to be had in studying foods, their origins and the processes involved in making, refining, harvesting and transporting them. As well as food there are other commodities like rubber, textiles, oil and paper which are interesting to investigate. Studies in geography may also be linked to sport.

Try to develop the habit of looking with the eye of a geographer when you go on days out. Why did this town or village grow up where it did? What do people do for a living in this area? In holiday locations you could consider the effect of tourism on the area. Are there any problems caused by visitors? There are often conflicts of interest between tourists, the local community and the conservation lobby which provide thought-provoking material for study.

Taking a global viewpoint, it's useful to make profiles of a selection of different countries in the world. You could start with a big outline map which you colour in each time you study a country. The individual studies can be as brief or as full as you wish. Alternatively, you might like to have the same format for each country, perhaps starting with an outline map, a drawing of the country's flag, then population, main industries, main cities, typical climate, main animals and plants, different kinds of landscape found there, any famous people from that country and so on, plus some interesting facts about each country. There are lots of opportunities for drawing for the artistically inclined student in studies of this nature.

Reluctant writers need not find this kind of project depressing as much can be recorded through maps and pictures. You could use the search engines on the internet to find information about each country. *National Geographic* magazine is an education in itself and reading newspapers regularly will help learners to absorb much geographical fact and information almost without noticing it. Travel sections of weekend newspapers often have fascinating pictures and articles about unusual places to visit. Helping to plan and research family holidays is another way of learning geography.

Studying the features of the local area can be a worthwhile practical activity. The geology of the area may make the landscape distinctive, for example if it has been subject to glacial activity or if it is a chalk or limestone landscape.

Trevor says:

What struck me when I first looked carefully at a GCSE geography textbook was how much of the work we had already touched on informally through the boys' observations and questions. We have done some projects including one on the weather and another on coal and mining. Also, we have often had lively discussions about all sorts of issues that affect the local community, including the location of a new shopping mall and the effect that it had on the local traders, the closure of a major car factory and its impact on employment locally and also the issues around the building of new housing estates in the area. The boys have always been fascinated by transport and travel and we have watched planes at a major airport near us and taken lots of interest in the movement of lorries on motorways.

We discuss issues in the news which are further from home, too, including earthquakes and floods, as we have always encouraged a global perspective.

GCSE is available to private candidates, but whether or not you are planning to take the exam you might like to consider doing some practical work to add interest to your studies. There are lots of projects that can be completed without special equipment or resources. Here are some examples:

- A study of office location in a town or city. Choose an area to study that is not too large. Draw a map and record the location of office premises. Identify and record the different types of offices. Look at changes of use in the area over the last twenty years: the library should be able to help with town maps showing individual properties. Draw conclusions based on the numbers, types and locations of offices and the changes that have taken place, and record them.

- A comparative study of two country parks. Visit both parks and find out as much as possible about both of them. Collect maps, pictures and information. Size? Average number of visitors per week? Average length of visit? (You will need to interview visitors leaving the parks to find this out.) Cost of entry? Catchment area from which visitors come? Amenities at each? Educational facilities and programmes? Number of staff employed? and so on.

- A farm study. Investigate the possibility of visiting a farm near you. Find out about the location and history of the farm. Take photographs and draw maps of land use. Prepare a questionnaire to find out if the farmer has changed land uses over the last ten years. Try to find out reasons why, and ask about any future proposals.

- A coastal study. If you live near to the coast, you could choose a stretch of coastline to study. Draw a map of the area. Identify as many plant and animal species as you can. Look at the type of rock and the geological structure of the area. Study the physical processes there: erosion, deposition, wave action. Investigate any special ecosystems like salt marshes. Investigate any human activities there and their impact on the area. Record your observations and include maps, sketches, photographs and diagrams in your study. A similar study could be carried out on a stretch of river if you are not near to the sea.

Any geography textbook will have similar examples which you can adapt and alter to suit your circumstances.

Information Technology (IT)

This subject is known as information and communication technology (ICT) in schools but it's interesting to note that, as far as we know, this title isn't used anywhere in the business world. IT may be studied at various levels and in different ways. If the young person isn't particularly interested in IT it's reasonable to adopt a practical approach and integrate it with other subjects. Keyboard skills and familiarity with the fundamental principles of computing are useful starting-points. Work in other areas of the curriculum may involve word processing, use of the internet and email, graphics and perhaps some use of presentation software. Database and spreadsheet packages are in common use everywhere in the world of work and it makes sense to gain some idea of what they do.

You could plan some projects using spreadsheets and databases which will be of practical use in the home in order to gain some experience with the software. For instance, the family's address book could be put into a database, including information about children and birthdays. It's also useful to investigate printing labels for Christmas cards. A database might also be used to list and classify a CD collection, or to keep track of the library books! Young people could use a spreadsheet to keep records of savings and expenditure. These are simple uses of the software but they involve real things. You will probably use your computer's capabilities naturally in all sorts of other areas of the curriculum, and any experience is useful.

If your learner decides to take IT seriously you might want to invest in some suitable hardware and software. If you plan to buy a new computer it makes sense to get a multimedia computer with a modem and as much disk space and memory as you can afford. It's surprising how quickly computers reach the limits of their capabilities when you move on to more complex tasks. You will also need either an inkjet or a small laser printer. Inkjet printers are relatively cheap to buy but the consumables are expensive if you do any quantity of printing. Laser printers are dearer to buy but some are very cheap to run.

A microphone for sound input and a scanner would both open up many possibilities; access to a digital camera and datalogging equipment would be useful but certainly not essential. HEAS has datalogging equipment which is available for loan to subscribers. You would need word processing software, presentation software and also database, graphics and spreadsheet packages. Modern word processing software has most of the features that desktop publishing offers so the latter is not nearly as important as it was when word processing was less sophisticated than it is today. Control equipment and software would be interesting but not essential. The important thing is to understand the principles by investigating these areas of IT even if it's not possible to gain access to this part of the technology to do practical work. This can come later at college if the young person wants to specialize in IT. Some of the computer magazines on the market give away free demonstration versions of a range of software on CD, and you can learn quite a lot about unfamiliar software by making use of these.

Getting to know the software may seem a bit daunting to adults but interested young people will usually play with it and find out a lot about it in an apparently random fashion if they are given enough access to it. This is possible for home educators as they are not subject to the constraints of the school timetable. This process may become very rapid after they have had the chance to investigate several different applications thoroughly.

The investigative approach gives confidence and a depth of knowledge about general principles which is fundamental to the development of good IT skills. IT professionals have said that young people who have just started work often blame the software at work for not being able to do what the software at school did. They don't seem to realize that the unfamiliar software may be capable of doing the same thing but in a slightly different way. This may highlight a danger of the school approach; in spite of the emphasis on practical skills and 'hands-on' methods, it seems that there may be a passivity about work in 'ICT' which doesn't help young people to acquire skills which are transferable to other contexts.

There are many interesting aspects of IT which may be tackled at home. You may like to make a multimedia presentation about an interest, or about the family. As well as their use for accounting, spreadsheets may be used to investigate other variable data. Some examples might include the nutritional content of recipes, the cost of meals or the nature and volume of traffic at a nearby location at certain times of the day or week. There are books available which give examples and detailed instructions for the different uses of spreadsheets.

Database software can be used for recording and analysing information of many different kinds. Some young people like to build up a database of information about their favourite singers and bands or about hobbies such as cars, aeroplanes or wildlife. More extended projects could involve designing questionnaires for collecting data, entering this into a database, forming hypotheses and testing them, using reports and queries, producing graphs and making a report on the findings.

Many young people enjoy making a website about themselves and their interests. In the process they may get involved with all sorts of interesting things including programming in HTML and using Java-Script. Again, there are good books which are easily available to help with learning in these areas. There are also courses available on the internet, including some information which is free to download.

The internet may be very useful for finding information on every conceivable subject. Parents must decide for themselves how much supervision they should exercise over their child's explorations of the world wide web, but searches which are undertaken together provide good opportunities to discuss the information and make a critical evaluation of its usefulness. Many home educators make a lot of use of email as a means of keeping in touch and making friends. Also there is the question of computer security, particularly the nature and effects of viruses and ways of protecting your computer against them including firewalls and anti-virus software.

If you have more than one computer at home you could consider networking them with a network kit. This would be a useful exercise that would give some insight into computer networks and it would enable you to share a printer. It also makes it much easier to move data from one machine to another.

There is also the option of doing many interesting projects away from the computer that would help young people to discover more about some of the complex uses of IT in the business world. You could make a study of the Data Protection Act and the ways in which it is enforced, looking at the rights which it gives to individuals and the responsibilities which it gives to organizations which hold information. You could also investigate the technology of bar codes, loyalty cards and stock recording systems. Family and friends may be useful sources of information as you could ask them about the ways in which IT is used in their places of work. Computer magazines are also good for finding out about many different aspects of IT in business and they are a useful way of keeping up to date with advances in technology and computer-related issues.

All of the areas mentioned above would be a good preparation for work at GCSE level, and the exam is available to private candidates. If the learner is keen to do GCSE Information Technology it would be a good idea to get some practice for the coursework by planning and carrying out an extended project which involves solving a problem using a range of software. Coursework for IT involves systems design and implementation and all the necessary documentation for the system. It may be very time-consuming to complete and it's advisable to ensure that the young person is familiar with the applications used before beginning the coursework task.

Design and technology

Parents embarking on home education really need to ask themselves some questions about design and technology. First of all, what is this subject all about? How can we study design and technology at home? Alternatively, do we really want to, and what other options do we have instead?

What is design and technology? For many parents this subject is a complete mystery. It simply didn't exist when they were at school and now it has appeared as the fourth subject in the national curriculum hierarchy, coming next in importance after English, maths and science. In essence, design and technology is composed of elements of the former practical subjects of cookery, needlework, woodwork, electronics and metalwork which have been integrated in a manner which emphasizes design, factory processes and production methods. The *national curriculum Handbook for Secondary Teachers in England* states in a side-note to the subject:

> During Key Stage 3 pupils use a wide range of materials to design and make products. They work out their ideas with some precision, taking into account how products will be used, who will use them, how much they cost and their appearance. They develop their understanding of designing and making by investigating products and finding out about the work of professional designers and manufacturing industry. They use computers, including computer-aided design and manufacture (CAD/CAM) and control software, as an integral part of designing and making. (Department for Education and Employment and Qualifications and Curriculum Authority, 1999, p. 136)

At Key Stage 3 pupils in school study all the different areas but pupils working towards GCSE at Key Stage 4 specialize in one area. GCSE courses are offered in the different options of Electronic Products, Food Technology, Graphic Products, Resistant Materials Technology, Systems Control Technology and Textiles Technology.

How can we do this at home? With some imagination and some ideas from a textbook or two, design skills may be developed and practised very well at home. The principle of design is a popular area for study and there are innumerable sources of inspiration in daily life once you have developed the ability to see the potential in everyday objects. On a more technical note, CAD software is accessible at home for your home computer from around £50–£100. You can learn all about the properties of materials and components and you can study and find out a lot about making products and industrial production processes.

It's not essential to gain hands-on experience of control systems and technology at home because you can learn about the principles and investigate control systems in everyday life. Health and safety regulations prevent most factories from allowing under-16s to visit them but some larger companies have viewing areas, promotional videos and information which describes their industrial processes. Some companies have an annual open day when the public may visit and take part in a guided tour of the factory. Alternatively, you may be able to find someone among your family and friends who could arrange a private visit at a quiet time to see factory systems in operation. It's also possible to find out a lot about the processes by asking people to explain what happens in their factory.

There are textbooks available which have been written to be used with the design and technology curriculum, and you could work through these and study them. Many of the design activities can be tackled at home, and it's possible for the student to do enough practical work and study at Key Stage 3 in order to prepare for work at GCSE level. Design and Technology is available to private candidates but depending upon the option which you choose for study at GCSE, it may be advisable to consider doing a course at a further education college in order to make it easier to complete the practical work.

Do we really want to study design and technology at home? Lesley's views are shared by many parents:

> We are very sceptical about the value of design and technology as it is taught in schools. For us the most serious issue is that of food technology. Cookery used to be taught in a way that was relevant to pupils as they used to learn about nutrition, healthy meals, budgeting, planning and preparing meals for different occasions and for different people, kitchen hygiene and care, as well as other interesting things like making cakes, pastry and biscuits. Now the cookery part of the course seems to have been given over mainly to cookery as a manufacturing process. The pupils are asked to design cook-chill meals for the supermarket and snack foods for teenagers. They have to design packaging and batch processes to ensure the quality and uniform size of their 'products'.
>
> What kind of message is this sending to an entire generation of young people about fast food and processed meals? Now that so many mothers are out at work as well, schools can't assume that young people are learning the art of cooking at home. We are at risk of seeing the next generation reach adulthood with the notion that cooking is about warming up processed foods.

Now they are being educated at home our teenagers are

becoming really enthusiastic about cookery. They plan and cook family meals and they make bread, soup, cakes and food for special occasions. We have made marmalade and strawberry jam and the results were really special. I don't want them to leave home without having experienced the creative side of cookery as well as the practical aspect of cookery as a life skill.

Moira takes a practical view:

We don't include design and technology as such in our home education, but we cover all sorts of practical things anyway. We work with wood and fabrics, we cook and sew, we make model boats and aeroplanes from plans that my husband had when he was a teenager and we have a keen interest in how things work. Much is said about design and technology giving young people confidence in their design skills, but we think that the most important thing at this stage is to encourage creativity in all sorts of different ways. Details of factory processes and industrial practices can come later – children don't need to be involved with all that as it will probably have changed completely by the time they get there anyway!

There are other options including many creative, practical and useful projects that may be undertaken at home using a hands-on approach. As well as cookery young people could investigate nutrition, menu planning and budgeting, healthy eating, creative cooking and food hygiene. Learners could study textiles, fashion, the history of costume; practical sewing projects could include making soft toys, children's garments, needlepoint, tapestry and so on. The young person might also like to do a project on new and smart materials, for instance synthetic microfibres, carbon fibre, neoprene, materials treated with thermochromic dyes using liquid crystal technology and many others.

Woodwork projects all give the opportunity for designing, choosing the type of wood, costing, using tools, practising measuring, cutting, joining, finishing, sanding, staining, varnishing and painting.

There are practical electronics projects that can be done at home and there is also much that can be learned about more specialized areas such as circuit boards and their components, silicon chip technology, logic gates, electronic control systems and their uses in everyday life. Even metalwork can be experienced at home. For instance, you can learn about the different metals and their properties and uses, and the principles of soldering; it's possible to experiment with soldering at home using copper pipe and a butane cylinder with a blowlamp attachment. Adult supervision would be essential, together with careful attention to safety! You could perhaps visit a blacksmith if there is one near you. Many young people learn about the principles of welding and discover about car body repairs, finishing and rust treatment. If you ask around among friends and contacts you may be able to arrange a visit to a garage if the young person is interested in car or motorcycle mechanics and maintenance.

All the above would give useful practical experience to young people which in turn gives them confidence in tackling new challenges.

Art

Drawing, painting and many different forms of art can be enjoyed at home simply as a creative activity, not as a 'school' subject. It's good to work with as many different materials and techniques as possible. Materials which you can build up gradually at home include coloured pencils (both the dry and the water-based kinds), pastels and oil pastels, charcoal, pencils for sketching, glass paint, acrylic paint, clay and other modelling materials. Coloured paper and card of different weights, fabric and wool scraps for collage, glues and scissors, pots and a collection of brushes may be added to your art equipment gradually.

Watercolour paints are relatively cheap to buy but the techniques of watercolour painting are harder to master than those of oil painting. Watercolour paint in tubes gives much better results than the blocks of colour in the standard paintbox, and you can mix from a fairly limited range of basic colours. Watercolour paper gives the best results as thinner paper buckles and goes lumpy when it gets wet. Stretch the watercolour paper first by wetting it, then tape it firmly to a board with gummed paper tape on all four sides. Leave it to dry completely before use.

Oil painting is more expensive, but you can start with just a few tubes of colour and you don't need to buy special board for your paintings. It's cheaper to use big sheets of hardboard cut up into smaller pieces, sealed with diluted PVA glue or wallpaper paste and painted with two coats of white matt emulsion paint. There are some good art courses available in books and on videos which give a basic introduction to the different techniques. If your child is drawn to art naturally you may find that you don't have to do much apart from providing the materials and some ideas from time to time. Or you may enjoy painting and drawing together.

If the young person wants to take art more seriously, perhaps with a view to GCSE later on, you may wish to pursue the subject in more depth. There is a great deal of varied and interesting art that can be done at home at this stage, starting with the materials mentioned above. Have a look in the library for big, lavishly illustrated books on the history of art; these will be invaluable to consult as you go along. In time the young person might appreciate some professional input through an art evening class or a summer course, but there is much to be done at home as well. As with other areas of special interest home educators have the opportunity to spend as much time on art as they wish, and the rest of the curriculum can be arranged around it if necessary.

Experience of a variety of practical art projects is essential if success in exams is a goal; although young people often have a marked preference for a particular aspect of art it's necessary to develop the ability to work easily and confidently using a range of different materials and styles.

One very important piece of equipment is the sketch book. It's helpful to have it to hand as often as possible in order to capture a good idea when it comes along, and also to record interesting details, textures, shapes and so on when you are out visiting different places and looking at life with the artist's eye. Work in the sketch book is done quickly with the aim of developing fluency, ease and speed in recording ideas and impressions.

It's good to gain some experience of three-dimensional art using clay and other modelling materials. Models made in clay can be air-dried if you don't have access to a kiln, and you could also use Newclay or any of the other modern modelling materials which are satisfying to work with and clean to use. Once you have the idea for your model, make some preliminary sketches from different angles and think about the techniques that will be needed to make it. Practise joining slabs of clay by tooling the edges together and experiment with building up curved shapes by using tooled coils of clay. Use a wet sponge and try various ways of smoothing, decorating and finishing the surface of the model. These traditional techniques work with Newclay as well as with red clay, but if you're using air-dried red clay do remember that your models must be kept dry! They will not withstand water unless they have been kiln-dried.

Modelling may be done alongside sketching of three-dimensional objects to sharpen the powers of observation. Collect interesting objects and make arrangements of unusual items, sketching them from different angles. Aim to work quickly and concentrate on catching the overall impression that you see. Try using a desk lamp to give a strong light source and move it around to give different effects. Experiment with objects that have a variety of different textures. Try concentrating on the space around the objects and drawing the edge of the space instead of the objects – you will see them differently if you do! This line of enquiry might be pursued out of doors by making studies of skylines, buildings, spaces between buildings, railings, fences, steps, archways, bridges and other features.

Work might continue in several directions from here. There is a rich area for discovery associated with art and the environment, both the built environment and the natural world. The world of architecture is full of interesting studies on both a large and a small scale. How is space used in big buildings? What is the relationship between the shape of the building and its purpose? What mood is created by the use of the space? Think about a church, a concert hall, a shopping mall, railway stations old and new (why have they changed?), a museum and so on. On a smaller scale look at shapes, patterns, textures, details, decorations, lines; try to be on the alert for interesting details from ground level up to as high as you can see.

Then there is a huge range of projects associated with landscapes of different kinds. Using a simple viewfinder – a sheet of card with a rectangular hole cut in it – helps to focus the attention on the composition of the view for the sketch. Look for views that present contrasting elements, perhaps contrasting natural objects with man-made ones. If an interest develops you could look at landscapes in art history and consider their different moods and how they were created. Some young artists enjoy interpreting landscapes from descriptions in literature and poetry. There are examples everywhere; try Wordsworth's *Prelude*, for instance, or for a fantasy landscape look at Coleridge's 'Kubla Khan'.

Moving on, you could look at perspective and light: look at early works of art, for example medieval wall paintings, illustrations from medieval manuscripts, early church art and so on and compare with the post-Renaissance 'modern' sense of perspective and scale. Contrast these with the fragmented and overlapping views of cubist art with its conflicting sources of light and limited colour range. Look at perspective in art from other cultures for comparison, and discuss the different perceptions behind these. Experiment with some cubist art of your own.

Try some designs of your own based on art from other parts of the world. Note interesting motifs, decorations, shapes, themes and uses of colour and experiment with them. Look for cross-cultural influences. Look at prehistoric and early art too, and think about how art conveys ideas and feelings. Some people find that their imagination responds to music, poetry and descriptive writing, so try using these as starting points for pictures, sketches or abstract work with colour to express mood and emotion.

Another area to be explored is art relating to portraiture. How do we perceive people? What different sides of their character do they show to us? How can we represent these characteristics in art, perhaps using colour and symbol? This is a line of enquiry that can be pursued independently of the techniques used for drawing faces and bodies, and it can be quite liberating to look at people in a new way. Many people are represented in poetry and literature, and some young artists like to realize their visualizations of these characters through art. The power and effect of masks is a related area which is worth exploring too.

There are many other areas of art that can be enjoyed at home including work with textiles, collage, photography and work with computer graphics and animation. You can also study different artists and their styles and the history of design.

Home educators have a distinct advantage when it comes to visiting art galleries and exhibitions. Individual family or small group visits tend to be much more beneficial than the school trip as they are quieter and more thoughtful and they may be geared to the specific interests of each student. Most places have educational materials that you can buy; some will have information which you can request in advance of your visit. Get in touch beforehand and ask for the Education Officer or for the Education Department, and see if they have any material which they would be able to send to you beforehand. Many museums have an internet website and some of these enable you to make a 'virtual' visit to see the collections. This may be very helpful in planning how to make the most of your visit. For older students who are committed to art and design, a visit to the Victoria and Albert Museum in London would be an inspirational experience.

GCSE Art is available to private candidates but do allow plenty of time for the coursework.

Music

When you are thinking about music as part of your home education you will need to decide on your priorities. The great advantage of home education is that you are able to respect your children's wishes, and the way that you approach the subject will depend on the level of involvement which they have with music.

If the young person is not musical and not interested there's very little point in pursuing the matter if they haven't shown any enthusiasm by the time they reach secondary age. There is no need at all to study it formally anyway and it would be sufficient to offer the child opportunities to listen to music from time to time. Young people often respond to the excitement and immediacy of live music, so it's worth watching out for opportunities to attend any concerts and performances locally. Experiencing a range of different kinds of music may help to spark off an interest. A very worthwhile aim in music is to try to encourage and develop the art of listening attentively.

Music is a universal human activity and although there are a few individuals whose appreciation is hampered by a sense of pitch that is not very well developed, most people find that there are kinds of music that they enjoy.

As well as discovering classical music young people may find that they have an interest in other genres, perhaps jazz or ethnic music. In addition to listening, if they are generally creative, artistic and imaginative but not specifically musical, they may like to explore music in a broader way. There are many interesting possibilities for finding out about the relationship between music and drama, for instance. One approach would be to study the effect of music in films and television programmes and to explore the different feelings that music can bring about in the listener. The history of the association between music and film, back to the early silent movies, might be another topic for research.

There are many ways of responding creatively to music and for some young people it's very rewarding to integrate it with other imaginative activities. Some young people enjoy using different kinds of music as a stimulus for creative writing or for dance routines, painting and artwork. For young people with an interest in history a study of the music of different historical periods may be enriching. Finding out about the music of other cultures may also be appealing to some. If you have access to the internet there is a lot of information out there which will help.

If an interest in learning a musical instrument emerges during these years it's possible to get them started on it at home. They will also need the basics of musical theory. There are many inexpensive books on the market which give a good introduction to the nuts and bolts of music, so this aspect of it may be catered for at home. The dilemma for the parent is whether to try to arrange lessons from the beginning or to wait to see if the interest is serious before paying for tuition. A certain amount depends on the instrument which the young person chooses. It's feasible to make progress on some instruments including the guitar, the recorder, the keyboard and the piano without formal tuition in the early stages.

It's more difficult to learn to play most of the orchestral instruments unless there is someone to help with fingering, strings, reeds, holding the instrument correctly and so on. Another young player who has got beyond the early stages may be able to give initial help and advice, but if the interest is more than just a passing whim it's important to get professional help before any bad habits set in.

There is also the question of making sure that the interest is serious before buying an instrument. Ideally it's good if you can borrow an instrument for a while in order to try it out, and sometimes friends may be able to help with this. Some music shops do a leasing scheme which enables parents to rent an instrument for a period to try it out. Then there is the option of paying for it after a certain time, with a proportion of the loan fees counted towards the purchase price. It's worth approaching the County Music Service as well as they are able to lend instruments in some cases, although the degree to which they are able to help home educators varies from area to area. Ask them for details of any choirs, orchestras, ensembles and workshops in the area as there may well be groups which home educated young people can join.

Some young people are already keen musicians by this stage and they may be making good progress on an instrument. They may wish to take up music seriously, and you may wonder how on earth you are going to nurture and encourage their talent at home. Parents are often anxious in case they spoil their children's chances by keeping them at home if they show interest and ability, but there are good arguments for saying that home has distinct advantages for the young musician particularly in the later years. Practice may be easier at home, for instance. If a child is at school it may be necessary to practise first thing in the morning, which may be anti-social as well as rather painful. And a tired child will not practise well after a busy day at school.

Home education allows for the curriculum to be arranged around the music, rather than the other way round. Composing is possible at home, either using a pencil and a pad of manuscript paper or using computer software and a keyboard. The latter is not essential but it takes the labour out of copying the parts of the composition for performance. Music specialists are not always in favour of early exposure to computer software for composing as it may cause young people to miss out on the foundations of the underlying musical theory.

As well as a rich variety of music there is a range of programmes on Radio 3 which explore different aspects of music and these are both educational and inspiring. Cable and satellite television has the Performance Channel which is available by subscription. As much time may be given to music as you and the young person feel is necessary. There is freedom from the powerful effects of peer pressure and the pop culture of school as well. All too often, musical teenagers are made to feel strange by their fellow pupils at school and this may have devastating effects. Some have even turned to home education because they have been bullied as a direct result of their interest in music.

Depending on where you live you may have to travel quite a distance to find the right instrumental teacher, but families who have chosen to do this are adamant that it's worth the effort in order to have the benefits of education at home. For teenagers who are committed and who have reached a good standard already it's reasonable to have lessons fortnightly or even monthly.

There are also opportunities for local music-making, music societies, summer schools, jazz groups, the County and National Youth Orchestras and Saturday classes at the various music colleges if you live near to them.

It has to be said that GCSE Music may be difficult to do at home as a private candidate. Part-time attendance at further education college, either pre- or post-16, may be a way round it but not all colleges offer the subject. You may find that you have to ask at various colleges before you find one that offers it, so it's crucial to make your enquiries early so that you can make the necessary arrangements. Most young performers who are interested in qualifications take the Associated Board exams. As well as the usual orchestral instruments, piano and so on, the Associated Board exams include jazz instruments and they are straightforward to arrange through a music teacher.

Young people may develop an interest in any kind of music at home, and home education may give them the opportunity that they need to break into this competitive world. This is Kelly's story:

> When I reached secondary age my parents decided that they didn't want me to go to secondary school. My mother taught me at home herself for a bit, then she got a tutor for me. I did lots of different things with my tutor as my interests changed and I liked learning that way. One thing that didn't change, though, was my interest in music, especially singing. One of my cousins played the guitar and I had a group of friends who also enjoyed singing, so we used to sing together and we made up our own songs as well. As time went on I got more and more interested, and I begged Mum and Dad for music lessons. I found a singing teacher and she helped me a lot. I love country music and I play it all the time at home and sing along to it.
>
> Then I had some chances to do some singing in public and I began to be interested in the possibility of getting into country music as a career. Mum and Dad were really supportive and encouraging although they wanted me to have a good education in case things didn't work out. They agreed to take me to the Country Music Fair in Nashville for our holiday one year and I had the time of my life. I even managed to sing there and that was it! I knew that I would have to try everything to make my dream happen, or I would never know .... .

I tried the Careers Service but they couldn't help me much and they didn't really know much apart from details of college courses in Performing Arts. So I searched the internet and found the website of a young performer who has a promising career. I emailed her and asked her how she got started. She put me in touch with her agent and he agreed to see me, and I sang for him. He was great and he liked what I did, so he has arranged for me to sing at quite a few different places. He has also given me some openings into country music journalism, and I now have my own column in a magazine and I do reviews of new CDs as well. I'm learning fast and everything is going well so far.

I'm looking at the possibility of doing a course at college as well, but I have to make sure that I'm free to follow up any performing opportunities that come my way, which are often at short notice. It's very exciting and I'm going to make the most of every opportunity. I know for certain that if I'd been in school none of this could have happened, so I'm incredibly grateful to Mum and Dad for their decision to educate me at home.

As we said at the beginning of this chapter, we do not want to be prescriptive. When you have taken your child through the secondary years you will be able to write your own account of how you did it, and it's sure to be unique to you.

CHAPTER 8

Social life

School and social development

First of all we must look at the question of the social aspect of school. School has come to be seen as an indispensable means of making friends and acquiring social skills. We think that there is a need to question a couple of widespread and fundamental assumptions about school. Are schools essential for social development? And what is the importance of the peer group?

The practice of sending children away from the home to learn in a specialized environment is prevalent in 'developed', industrialized Western-style societies. Older societies which are based on family and tribal models do not isolate their younger members in this way, and learning takes place naturally and informally within the rhythms of daily living. Thus children learn from older members of their society and they learn through play, by example and by doing. Social development is a natural process and the younger members are not kept apart from the world of the adults. Clearly the existence of school is not an absolute necessity for learning social skills as many societies manage perfectly well without it. It's a sobering thought that young people in tribal and family-oriented societies don't seem to have the same experience of alienation from their elders as some of our young people do. Is our society dysfunctional in that its members feel the need to push their children into pre-school education earlier and earlier in the belief that this is how they learn social skills?

Originally the rationale for school had nothing to do with learning social skills and making friends. Some people have argued that schooling for the masses was deemed necessary as an instrument of social control and the aim was to mould young people through drill and discipline into a compliant workforce which would obey authority. The connection between school and personal social development was not made until long afterwards, but people then began to attach great importance to the notion that children need to learn social skills by being forced to spend most of their waking hours with large numbers of other young people of the same age.

This assumption has become widespread in recent years, but is it correct? Perhaps it has come about through backwards reasoning: peer groups are universally experienced by children in school, therefore they must be somehow essential. Why? There are no situations in life where adults are expected to associate on a daily basis with thirty or so people of their own age. Adults mix in groups whose members have something in common, for instance skills and knowledge used in the workplace or interests and knowledge connected with hobbies and leisure pursuits. Adult groupings invariably involve people of different ages and different levels of experience. This allows for younger or less experienced members to learn from the others, but this is not the same for children in school.

Some young people are happy at school and they enjoy the social life for the most part, but others have to endure years of misery. One of the problems associated with peer groups in school is that young people are all struggling to some degree with the same confusions, anxieties and problems of growing up. The tensions within a group of school pupils may make it an intolerably hostile place for its more sensitive members. Such groups lack the balance which is found in typical mixed-age groupings of adults where more experienced members are able to show tolerance and understanding to others.

It's easy to see that the dynamics of peer groupings make them a breeding ground for negative feelings which are based on fear and uncertainty. A 16-year-old school pupil reports:

> Our school is small and pretty friendly as these places go. But even we aren't immune from problems. Last year a group of girls decided to have a go at P., a quiet girl who works hard and is nice to everyone. The ringleader of the group started to say that she was strange (the worst possible sin) and began a whispering campaign about everything she did – even the way she held her cup and the way she fiddled with her hair. I know now that P. isn't a bit strange but this was so powerful that you end up believing it. Looking back I can see that this group were projecting all their own anxieties on to her, and they made all sorts of jokes about her. It was awful as after a while everyone else was afraid to talk to P. in case they got the same treatment.
>
> Although I didn't actively join in with it, I must admit that I found it was impossible to stand out against it. It was all very subtle – not the sort of thing that you could really tell the tea-

chers about – and the staff had no idea about what was going on. I don't know how P. kept going, because it was horrible. Thank goodness it's different this year as a couple of the girls have left and P. has friends now.

Home educated children often have friends of their own age but they have the freedom to make their own connections. They aren't forced to associate with people whose values they don't share and whose company makes them unhappy. Talking to many young people who have been withdrawn from school has shown us that the pupil's view of school is very different from the adult's. Adults in school simply don't know what is going on and they can never share fully in the young person's experience of the interactions between the pupils.

What are social skills?

What are the social skills which children learn as they grow up? These are all to do with relating to other people including making friends, sharing, learning how to get on with others who are not friends, managing difficult situations and stress, being at ease with people, tolerating others, welcoming and including others, teamwork and working together, cooperation, competitiveness, assertiveness, conversation, considering the needs of others and caring for them, together with a range of appropriate social responses for different situations and so on. All of these responses develop over time as children mix with others, regardless of whether or not they attend school.

Educational psychologists and other education professionals are often to be heard in media interviews asserting confidently and decisively that home educated children are isolated and missing out on the experience of school. There is not a scrap of evidence to support these assumptions. No research study has ever concluded that home educated children are socially disadvantaged.

The range of social experiences which home educated children have is very varied. Some may have less social contact than they would in school but parents argue that quality is better than quantity. One characteristic that we have come across repeatedly is that children who are educated at home tend to have a range of friendships and social contacts across the different age groups. The effect of this is often seen in the ease with which these young people relate to adults. They are accustomed to responding to adults on equal terms rather than relating to them across the teacher–pupil divide in the artificial social construct of school.

So what actually happens when families go it alone at home?

Young children

Families find all sorts of things to do, either in the local community, with family members or with other home educators. Sheila has one child but he isn't lonely:

> We go out several times a week. We go to see Nan on Fridays and do her shopping, and sometimes Andrew stays with her while I go out. He might take a book or some work to do, or they might play games or watch a video together. We see people most days, either when we meet the other local home educating families or when we have friends round to play. Some evenings there are things like gym and football at the local sports centre, and there's Sunday School too and various camps during the holidays. We do work in the mornings mostly.

Andrea has younger children:

> Ours have their social life organized for them and they don't complain! We just pile into the car and go off to whatever is happening. There are several things going on each week including an art and craft workshop, a walk or a trip to the beach in the summer with friends and usually a meeting in someone's house as well.

David and Rhona's situation was unusual:

> When we took Julie out of school she was 9 and we were both working in the family business, which is a pet and garden centre on the edge of town. We did wonder if she would be lonely as she had to be with us during the day, but there was no choice in the matter as she couldn't carry on being so unhappy at school. She had her corner in one of the offices where she did her work and one of us was always around to stop and help if she needed it. Well, she settled down to it and got her work done, then she would go round and be in the shop and talk to the staff and she loved it. We kept in touch with some friends that she had made at school, and after school finished they would usually come round here on the way home. They would all go off to ride the horse and play around together. We didn't get much time for outings as a family but that's life ... and Julie wasn't exactly cut off from the world while she was home educated.

The teenage years

As they get older, young people become more independent and also more discriminating when it comes to social activities. They also begin to take charge of their own social life. These two families have always been home educators. Sandy found that things didn't work out as she had expected:

> I was a bit disappointed when I found that he didn't want to go to any of the local home educators' activities any more. He said that he felt awkward and too big and he preferred to be on his own. I had hoped that he would carry on going as he knew everyone so well, but it didn't work out that way. He says that he doesn't like being in a group any more, and he likes to go out with one friend at a time. He has several quite close friends of different ages and they're all nuts about computers.

Elizabeth recounts how the situation changed as her sons grew up:

> Both of mine found that they actually needed time to be on their own, and my older son says that he needed to be lonely for a bit to find out who he was. They both wanted to sort out their own social life. Suddenly I didn't need to drive them everywhere and I didn't have to make packed lunches several times a week. My younger son has a great friend who is in her 70s, and he often goes and visits her. They have lots to talk about – she got her first computer a year or so ago, and she also has two cats. He's so lucky to have a friend that he can really talk to and she's very wise and caring. He is also friends with other boys in their teens. His older brother is now at college and he's fitted in really well with the others.

If a young person has been withdrawn from school the position regarding social life may be different, as Naomi discovered:

> We took her out of school when she was 13 and it was about a year before she recovered her self-confidence. It was really worrying at first as she didn't want to go out and she hardly saw anybody for ages. She had a couple of friends from school but she wasn't keen on meeting new people, and it's only just recently that she's wanted to try new things. She's just joined a drama group and she's started going to a youth club with one of her friends.

It may be particularly hard for teenagers to make new friends especially if they have had unhappy experiences at school, and it may be difficult for them to adjust to being at home after years of being surrounded by people of their own age at school. They may feel lonely at home but they may not feel able to break into new social situations. Try to reassure them that things will change and that this awkward stage will pass. It's also worth pointing out that many young people in school feel very lonely and isolated in spite of being with others every day. If possible, help them to remain in contact with any friends from school. It's much better if you can help them not to lose touch, as re-establishing contact with former friends after a time may be too diffi-cult. It may be easier for them if you can suggest some sociable ac-tivities, perhaps swimming, bowling, meeting at a pizza restaurant for lunch or a trip to the cinema, to which they could invite their friends. Also, you could do some research into possible new activities in the area which young people might like to consider when they are ready. There may be clubs and groups out there for them to join when they feel a bit more confident after a while.

Home education and the family

Home education certainly has an effect on relationships within the family. Many parents find that they become closer to their children because of the time that they spend together, and parents often comment on the fact that they have remained friends with their children throughout the teenage years. Other parents report that life has been very difficult after they have withdrawn a child from school, but there has been no choice but to carry on.

Despite the unsubstantiated claims of professionals that young people who learn at home will be unable to separate from their parents later, we have found no evidence of any problems of this kind among home educators. We think that the reverse is true. Children who feel secure, valued and self-confident within the family seem to be more able to adjust to change and to new situations as they grow and ma-ture. Research with young children has shown that those in closer, more nurturant families are more independent outside the family, not less so (Lewis *et al.*, 1984).

Growing up at their own pace

In the same way as home educated children are able to make progress educationally at their own pace, it is possible for them to develop emotionally at a natural rate without having 'maturity' forced upon them by their peers at school. Joseph, a home educating parent, remembers:

> I had just started secondary school aged just 11. I had a friend from my primary school in my class and we were both very keen on cars. We both had collections of model cars and at first we

used to take some cars into school every day and play with them at break. We had only been there a couple of weeks when some older boys saw what we were doing and they made fun of us in a very hurtful way. I stopped playing with those cars on that day and I never played with them again, and I still remember how miserable I felt about it. My son is 12 and he still likes to play with Lego and with toy cars sometimes, but I know that he'll stop playing with them when he's ready and not because he's made to feel ashamed of his games.

Home educated children tend to meet and mix with many different individuals both in local home education groups and in other clubs and activities in the community; they are not leading sheltered lives as some critics believe. They have to learn to deal with difficult people and they have their share of disagreements, personality clashes and problems to handle. The difference is that emotional nurturing is possible at home. The parent may observe from a distance and help them to understand the hurts and problems in their relationships with others, only intervening if a situation becomes too much for them to handle. This 'apprenticeship' approach to learning social skills is a far more humane and profitable experience than the 'deep end' scenario of the school playground, where children have little guidance and support as they try to make sense of the situation. Perhaps this explains why people often remark on the self-confidence of home educated children.

Getting in touch with other home educating families is a good first step and the national organizations HEAS and EO both provide contact information for their members. You could telephone or write to families who live near to you and suggest an informal meeting, or you may find that there are local activities in your area at which you can meet others. There is a surprising variety of people who educate their children at home, so don't give up if you don't find like-minded families immediately with children of a similar age. It's a good idea to try to meet as many people as possible.

Starting a local group

If there are no meetings locally you might like to consider starting up some activities. To begin with you only need two or three families who are interested as a thriving local group may well grow from small beginnings. Many groups meet in each other's houses but if the group is successful it soon outgrows the facilities which the average home has to offer. Sometimes families decide early on that neutral ground is best, perhaps agreeing to meet regularly at a playground, a swimming pool or a leisure centre with different activities on hand.

There is a great variety of possible activities and the structure of local groups ranges from totally informal to highly organized. They tend to be very fluid indeed as they are based on the needs and the enthusiasms of the families who attend them. It's not unusual for local groups to flourish and then disappear altogether for a time if there is no longer a need for them. Fortunately the national organizations provide continuity as they help families to make contact with one another, and a new group may emerge overnight if a few families wish to start something up.

There are many things that you can do if there is a group of families who are enthusiastic about organizing events. Usually it's possible to arrange anything that a school group could do if there is enough commitment and support among the local families. This might mean sports including swimming, football, basketball, athletics, tennis, badminton, gym, skiing, cooperative games and parachute games. Drama and dance may also be possible, and many groups arrange outings including concerts, ballet, theatre and opera performances. There may be matinée performances and events for schools to which a local home educators' group may gain access at a reduced price for a 'school' group.

There are also visits to nature reserves, historical reenactments, heritage sites, parks and playgrounds, museums and places of interest perhaps including a police station, pizza restaurant, fire station or a supermarket. Walks and picnics are free and very companionable ways of giving the children opportunities to make friends. Everything depends on the level of interest of the families who meet regularly. It has to be said that arranging any regular activities which involve input from a paid specialist, for example a swimming teacher or a sports coach, are unlikely to be successful unless there is a well-defined local group in existence to provide continuity and an input of new members when children move on.

Informal groups may meet at a well-known place, perhaps in the foyer of a museum or in a shopping centre, on the same day and time each week or each month. New families who hear about the get-together may just come along and see if anyone else happens to be there at the meeting-place at the usual time. This simple, low-key arrangement has the advantage that it requires no organization and no structure and there is no need for a committee, for funds or for means of communication. It provides a means of making contact with others which doesn't require any commitment, and it forms a meeting-point where families might get together to arrange a group meeting for another occasion. This kind of arrangement does have the disadvantage, though, that the range of activities which are open to the families involved is fairly limited.

Families in some areas have a 'telephone tree' which is a means of passing information quickly round a group of parents. Each person on the tree undertakes to telephone the same two or three other families each time if there is information to pass round the group about a meeting or a local event. This spreads the work of communication and involves everyone in the task, but it does need one person who is willing to manage the system by adding new families to the tree and removing those who no longer want to be involved.

The structure and degree of organization of a local group often evolves over time, beginning with a very informal arrangement and gradually developing a structure as the need arises. Once there have been some enjoyable meetings, a group of families often becomes very enthusiastic about the results. They may decide to broaden the scope of their activities by getting to know other families, and a larger number of members brings more possibilities to the group. Many educational group activities require a minimum number of children, and also a larger and more diverse group of parents brings with it additional energy, expertise and ideas.

The pattern that we have seen in very many long-established local groups over the years usually involves a nucleus of a few very committed families who are prepared to undertake the tasks of organizing and planning activities, getting other people involved and communicating with others, often via a local newsletter or list of events. As time goes by different families take over these tasks and the character of the group changes slightly as the individuals change.

Up and down the country home educators are quietly getting on with an amazing variety of activities, and there is a formidable amount of totally voluntary effort going into arranging initiatives which bring families together. In recent years there have been several national conferences for home educators and an annual home educators' seaside camp in the south of England. There are several Christian organizations and recently a new Muslim charity has been set up. There are local groups both large and small, both formal and informal, in all parts of the country and there are several internet websites which have been created by home educators in the UK. As well as all the activities which we have noted above, home educated young people in different local groups have enjoyed a huge variety of enterprises including sailing weeks on a Thames barge, working holidays on a farm project in the West Country, Duke of Edinburgh's Award schemes run by several groups, working on a tree-planting project in Essex which won an award, visits to the Millennium Dome, visits to the Royal Opera House and the Globe Theatre and attendance at the Royal Society Science lectures. Home education has come a long way since the days when families had to travel across several counties to meet others, and it shows no signs of diminishing.

CHAPTER 9

Special educational needs

Many children with special educational needs (SEN) have a good experience of school, either in a mainstream setting or in a special school. For others the experience of schooling is not at all beneficial. This chapter is for parents who have doubts and who want to know more about the option of home education for their child. The information is necessarily of a very general nature as it's not possible to comment in detail in this book on the range and complexity of situations involving SEN. Children with SEN who are home educated have a range of needs. Some are severe and others are mild; sometimes the special need is a short-term problem and in other cases it's permanent. Very often the problem may not be severe or specific enough to warrant a statement of SEN and in consequence the parents have failed to get any help for their child.

Education authorities in the UK are obliged by law to identify and assess children who might have SEN. They have the duty to make a statement of special educational needs (or Record of Needs in Scotland) if the assessment shows that the child has SEN. The statement defines the provision which the education authority is obliged to make for the child, but it doesn't prevent parents from educating the child at home if they wish to do so.

In our conversations with parents we have found that education and health professionals have widely differing views on the suitability of home education for children with SEN. Some are opposed to it, claiming that specialist teaching is essential. Another common assumption is that the child will be lonely at home without a social life and without the stimulus of other children. Others are very much in favour of education at home and they may recommend home education to families – usually off the record – as a good option. One parent said recently:

The head teacher telephoned me when she received my letter saying that I was taking my son out of school. She was very honest and encouraging and she said that between ourselves it was the best possible thing I could have done.

Another parent was told privately by her child's class teacher that it was completely impossible to give her son the individual attention he needed in the busy classroom.

Two contrasting accounts, involving children of different capabilities with Down's syndrome, show that the learning environment and the amount of individual input may be critical for children with SEN. Mrs P. was a highly dedicated, skilled and caring teacher who had a little girl with Down's syndrome in her small primary class. There was some debate as to whether the little girl should be placed at a special school but Mrs P. was keen to keep her with the other children. She taught the little girl all sorts of skills, mostly in her own time, and she succeeded in retaining her in her class for several years. When the girl reached the age for secondary transfer it became impossible to keep her in the school any longer and she was sent to a school for children with moderate learning difficulties in the next town.

At this end of her time with Mrs P. the child's speech had improved greatly and she loved looking at books. She took great delight in being useful by doing simple tasks like handing round materials and collecting up the other children's work. She was a very happy and sociable member of the class. Some months afterwards Mrs P. went to visit her in her new school. She was horrified to find that the girl seemed totally demoralized by her surroundings. Her speech had deteriorated and she had lost all the skills she had learned. At that time, neither the teacher nor the parents knew that home education was an option.

The second account is of Polly, a little girl with Down's syndrome who lived in a rural area in the South East. Her parents noticed early on that she responded well to lots of interest and individual attention, and they were concerned about the effect that school would have on her progress. They knew that no school could give her the amount of one-to-one help that she had been receiving at home in the early years. They decided to work with her at home instead of sending her to school and they both devoted themselves to a daily programme of activities with her. One thing that was lacking was some social life so Polly's father, a builder, built a swimming pool and a play area in the garden. The family invited all the children in the village to play and to use the pool, and their house was open to all. Polly enjoyed their company and continued to make good progress throughout her childhood. Later on her parents were delighted when Polly passed her driving test.

Inclusion of special needs children

The current climate of thinking emphasizes inclusion and a commitment to the principle of mainstream education for children who have SEN. In England and Wales, the Code of Practice on the Identification and Assessment of Special Educational Needs gives guidance to LEAs and schools on their duties and states that most pupils will have their needs met in mainstream schools without a statutory assessment. Although it is right that all children should have equality of opportunity many parents don't want mainstream education for their child. Their awareness of their child's all-round needs makes some parents deeply unhappy about it. Sally says:

> I know that she's got to live in the world when she grows up, but I can see that it will take me the rest of our time in mainstream education to prepare her for it. She can't cope with school. She hasn't got a clue about what's happening. She gets a classroom assistant for one hour a week but what use is that? She needs someone at her side all the time so that she can understand what's expected of her. She spends all her time at school getting anxious because she's slow to catch on to what's happening around her. No one has time to help and all the children just push past her and leave her behind. She can learn but not under those conditions. I get so angry when I hear all the current talk about enabling children with learning difficulties to stay in the mainstream. That's not equality – that's putting children like mine at a disadvantage unless proper provision can be made for them.

Some parents consider that neither mainstream nor special education would be right for their child, and home education may offer a third way for these families.

Withdrawing your child from school

When children who have statements of special educational needs attend ordinary mainstream schools in England or Wales, the procedure for withdrawing them is the same as that given on p. 6 of Chapter 1. The statement of SEN doesn't make any difference as it doesn't remove your right to educate your child in accordance with your wishes.

An exception does occur for pupils who are registered at a special school. If you decide on withdrawal, you will need to seek the LEA's permission to do so. This requirement is intended to act as a safeguard to protect the interests of children with special educational needs; it is not intended to be discriminatory and the LEA is not allowed to refuse their permission 'unreasonably'.

Giving information to the LEA

The LEA will probably ask for information about your educational arrangements at some stage. Heather recounts her experience of the Adviser's first visit:

We had been educating Zachary at home for nearly a year when I got a letter from the Adviser who works in this area. I agreed that he could come and visit us, but I felt very nervous about it. I knew that he wasn't a special needs Adviser and I wondered if he would understand what he was seeing. There was very little conventional work to show him as Zachary simply can't do what other 6-year-olds do. Our patient work over a year has meant that Zachary can now sit down and write his name on a piece of paper. He has learned some basic social skills and he has experienced a range of hands-on activities, and he can now get dressed by himself.

I knew it would be difficult to give an adequate impression of how we had spent our time over the past year, so I thought about the best way to prepare for the visit. I wrote down an account of the goals that I had in mind for the year for Zachary when we first started home education, then I made notes on the progress he has made towards our goals. Over the year we had taken photographs of special times and they provided evidence of what we've been doing together. I'm particularly pleased with the way he is learning to mix more easily with other children, and the photographs show how well he is doing.

I got out the leaflets from the places that we've visited and Zachary was keen to show them to the Adviser. We also have a big scrapbook of words and pictures that we work on together so we got it ready to show him. I also made a list of the different videos, television programmes and educational software that Zachary has been enjoying, together with the books that I have been reading to him. I was all prepared to defend my approach but the Adviser was fine.

Breda's daughter, Carol, has behaviour problems and dyspraxia:

Carol was very traumatized by failure at school and I withdrew her when she was 11. Carol's special needs had never been formally assessed but she was troubled and unhappy, and it needed a lot of time and patience before she settled down at home. If anybody remotely 'official' came to the house she would get very anxious and disturbed. I explained to her that someone would want to know about her education one day, and the idea of this seemed to trouble her a lot. I'm still not sure if she really understood what I was saying. Most of our home education is very active and Carol learns best by doing things. She makes models and she loves to work with wood and clay, and occasionally she will do some writing, mainly poems. She uses the computer too and she loves crafts.

Months went by, then one day the letter arrived. The LEA wanted to send someone to see us the following week. I postponed the first appointment as it fell on Carol's birthday, and when we talked about it I could see that she was very upset and worried about the visit. She didn't want to see the Adviser and she didn't want me to show him any of her work either. This put me in a very difficult position, but I hoped that the Adviser would understand if I explained the situation. I phoned him and offered to provide a full report in writing, which he accepted.

I went into considerable detail in the report, giving an account of the work that we do and describing some of the topics that we are covering at home. I noted the progress that I had observed as well. Carol also has a special needs tutor who visits us once a fortnight, and she wrote a report on her observations. I enclosed copies of educational and psychological assessments which we had arranged privately. In my covering letter I explained that I was unwilling to subject Carol to further stress and that I could not go against her wishes by forcing her to submit her work for inspection.

I was thankful to receive a courteous letter from the Adviser in reply which acknowledged our hard work and congratulated us on our arrangements. Thanks to HEAS he was aware that the law doesn't give LEA officials any authority to insist upon a visit to the home or to ask for access to the child, and he was willing to accept my information as evidence of satisfactory education.

Advantages of home education

Home education may not be the right way forward for every child with SEN but it does have many advantages. Parents have specific knowledge of the child's needs and they can match the home education to the child's rate of progress which may be slow. The child won't have to suffer the anxiety of feeling left behind by other members of the class. Sometimes an appropriate education is only available at a boarding school miles away but this may be too unsettling for the child. Parents usually find that it's possible to arrange any special training privately, for example Braille or sign language. If the child is exhausted through illness you can make the most of the 'good' times if education is taking place at home. It's also possible to work at unusual times if that suits the child best, and you can work for short periods with many breaks if necessary.

The social life of school often poses insuperable problems especially if the child has any emotional and behavioural difficulties. Helping children to learn social skills may be done very effectively from home as you can give them the assistance and support which they need in a variety of situations, perhaps in association with a group of home educators. Social life may be introduced very gradually at first and more may be undertaken as their skills develop. You can put time and effort into helping them to learn appropriate social behaviour, explaining problems and intervening if necessary. If you are there you can avoid the risk of bullying, and it often helps to communicate something of the child's difficulties to other children and to their parents to help them to understand the child's responses.

When you are learning at home you can take all the time that you need to overcome any fears, for instance the fear of water or swimming. Also you can take care over the child's environment, making any alterations to the home to provide the best possible conditions for learning and for good health. If necessary you can watch for and avoid any known allergens and take care over the child's diet. Some children tend to be over-excitable, and it's much easier to maintain a calm atmosphere at home. Learning at home takes the pressure off the child and you also have the scope to pursue a quiet and tactful investigation of the cause of the problems if this is not known already. One thing that you should bear in mind, though, is that you will not be able to ask for any financial or other help from the LEA. You will have to bear the costs of any special arrangements or training and the LEA will not normally pay for any private assessments or examinations.

Educational arrangements for children with SEN at home are very varied. Sometimes a carefully structured education is required, with plenty of repetition to reinforce basic skills before moving on. Enjoyment, a gentle pace of learning, progress in small, linked steps and plenty of experience of success may be priorities. For some children the education may be almost entirely practical with an emphasis on life skills, and for others informal education may be the best approach. Sometimes progress may be very gradual. Above all it's essential to be realistic about what the child may be capable of achieving so that you have some reasonable educational aims in mind.

Other children may be streets ahead of their peers in school when it comes to academic work and it may be a challenge to keep up with them and to maintain their interest. Variety may be particularly important and you may wish to introduce some subjects which are not

taught at school in order to broaden their experience. It's not un-
known for some children who have autistic tendencies, some degree of
Asperger's syndrome or a similar condition to show unusual competence in some areas, so it could be important to try out lots of different
things.

Families' stories

Sam had some real problems with reading and writing but he did not
have a statement of SEN. His mother tells us:

> Sam did go to school for the first two years but I soon realized that
> it wasn't working out. He was obviously bright and well motivated
> but I could see quite early on that he was struggling with writing,
> and his reading was not very fluent. Eventually I took him out of
> school because I could see that his enthusiasm was waning and I
> realized that matters would only get worse. We had to abandon
> everything associated with writing for some months, and I did a
> lot of reading to him instead of putting him under pressure to read
> for himself. I had to be very patient and it wasn't easy at all. He
> just couldn't make the connections between the sounds and the
> letters and he had great difficulty remembering the work we did
> on it.
>
> I was reluctant to use the term 'dyslexic' and he was very
> insistent that he didn't want to be labelled, but he does have great
> difficulty in this area. His reading did come on eventually and it
> was wonderful when he actually began to enjoy it and be excited
> by it. Writing remained a problem so we did lots of other things
> which didn't require it. When he was about 12 he began to show
> a talent for art, particularly pottery and all kinds of modelling. He
> really enjoyed his new-found creative interest and he also got his
> first computer at this stage. The computer became very important
> to him and his self-esteem improved quite a lot over the next
> couple of years.
>
> Then he decided that he wanted to go to college to take his
> GCSEs and at this point he agreed that we would have to find
> some strategies to help him with the writing and spelling problem.
> We used some dyslexia materials regularly for about a year and
> this did seem to help. We decided that the best way was to focus
> on the artistic and practical subjects and others which required
> the least possible amount of writing, so he took Maths, Physics
> and Art first of all. In the second year he took English and IT and
> he was so pleased when he passed, especially the English. It was a
> real struggle for him but he was able to go on to a two-year course

in Art and Design. I'm convinced that he would have given up entirely if he had stayed in school, but his problems weren't 'bad' enough for him to have received any learning support.

Mary was school phobic from an early age but her difficulties were never formally assessed. Mary's mother says:

We had problems right from the beginning. Mary's father left when she was 4 after things had been unhappy for some years. I planned to go out to work as soon as Mary started school and she seemed keen to go. She was quiet and small for her age but she was keen to learn. She made some friends but she wasn't happy at school and she began to have minor illnesses, but nothing that you could put your finger on. She used to cling to me at the school gate and it was horrible to have to leave her crying and frightened day after day while I went on to work. She told me later that she hated everything about the place, and she found it too noisy. The teachers were kindly and very puzzled about why she was so unhappy, but they were too busy to do very much for her.

The problems went on for years and she became withdrawn and very anxious. She had headaches, nightmares and all sorts of stress symptoms. She had more and more time off school and by the time she was 9 she had major problems. The education welfare officer became involved because in the end I just couldn't get her into school, and she used to call at the house every day to try to get her to go. One day Mary ran away and that was it. I realized that we couldn't go on and I kept her at home. I was threatened with court but just before matters got to that stage I heard about home education and I took her out of school.

Slowly she got her confidence back and she got stronger, and all the signs of stress disappeared. Learning at home suited her as she could be quiet and peaceful, and she loves to study and read and find things out. I feel angry and let down when I think of all those years when we struggled on with no help and the misery she suffered was unbelievable. I think the unhappy early years probably had repercussions when she first went to school, but there was never any offer of counselling or psychological help.

Thomas was visually impaired from birth and had a statement of SEN before he went to school. His mother turned to home education in desperation:

Thomas went to a special school when he was 5 as his sight was too poor for him to be able to cope in a mainstream school.

Everything went well until we moved house when he was 10, and he had to leave the school as it was too far for him to travel there. The only place that was available for him was at a special school in the borough which was supposed to be suitable for children with his disability. I accepted the place because I was assured that they had the facilities for him and he was there for a year.

I was horrified about the placement because there was no one at the school who has any training which is relevant to children with eyesight difficulties. I began to teach him Braille myself, which he had started to learn at his old school, because they had no teacher of Braille and they couldn't arrange for someone to come in to teach him. He learned nothing while he was at the school but they did a lot of playing. I withdrew him from the school three months ago and I'm still waiting to hear if I have permission to do so, but I have no intention of sending him back anyway.

Ned has some problems and he has a statement of SEN, but school wasn't the right environment for him. His father explains:

He's a very bright boy but we knew before he went to school that he would find it difficult. He does have behaviour problems which seem to be due to mild autistic tendencies, but he can relate to other people in his own way. He's affectionate, lively, curious, interested in things and very talkative, but he's completely obsessive and once he's made up his mind nothing will persuade him to change it. If he gets interested in something he has to go on with it until he decides he's had enough, and he will fly into a rage if you try to stop him. You can imagine that this didn't go down too well at school!

He's also afraid of some quite everyday things including dogs and sudden noises and he will run away without thinking if he is frightened. Once when he was at school he ran out to the other side of the playing field and he wouldn't come back into the classroom. The teacher had to drag him back indoors in the pouring rain and they were both soaking by the end of it. At first they thought he was naughty and we were made to feel that we had been too lenient with him, but some of his behaviour is bizarre and they quickly decided that he should be assessed. The statement said that he should attend a special unit in another school in the city which could cater for children with emotional and behavioural difficulties.

We visited the unit and we knew at once that it wasn't the place for him. So we took him out of school and he has been at home for nearly two years. His younger brother attends school and loves it, and we wouldn't want to take him out anyway as Ned is quite a handful. He's much quieter now than he was when he first came out of school as he was very disturbed by the whole experience, and academically he's really stretching us.

We meet with the local home educators for social life and they've been very good. On the whole they tolerate him well and they've come to understand his ways. I always have to be there with him in case things get too much, and the only real problems we've had are when we've been out on visits and trips with the group. Sometimes people at museums and other places are completely thrown by him especially if we haven't had a chance to have a word with them beforehand. But he's gradually getting the idea that what he does has an effect on other people, so we feel that we're making progress.

GCSE examinations and other qualifications

All the examining groups in the UK have policies and procedures to help candidates with SEN including arrangements for extra time, rest breaks and special versions of the question papers for candidates with visual or hearing impairment. Early discussion of the problems is essential, and it would be wise for home educators to make initial enquiries before candidates begin to study for their courses. You will need to provide evidence to support an application for special arrangements. Psychological and medical evidence may be required. A booklet containing guidance and information is published by the examining groups every autumn. It is sent to all examination centres and you should be able to obtain a copy by contacting one of the examining groups.

Further education colleges usually provide courses for people with varying degrees of special educational needs, and one of these may be a worthwhile option for young people who have been educated at home when they reach the age of 16. These courses encourage the development of a range of skills including personal and social education, communication skills, personal independence, health and fitness, personal empowerment and work skills. Some courses will lead towards nationally recognized qualifications.

CHAPTER 10

Options as children grow older

At this stage we do have to update our views on things that we knew about and it's necessary to review the assumptions that we have made for many years. It's noticeable that many parents still refer to 'O levels' when they enquire about home education! The qualifications field is not the only area which has changed out of all recognition in recent years and our knowledge, opinions and impressions may no longer be relevant to our young people.

Some parents may be at a loss to know how to advise a young person who has a particular ambition, and others may realize that independent advice would be helpful. The Careers Service may be able to assist. All young people, whether they are educated at home or at school, are entitled to a careers interview and advice.

Deciding the way forward

Some young people are well motivated and focused; they know what they want and they go and get it. These young people will need help, advice and encouragement from their parents but it's a positive process of finding out together. Other young people are not so fortunate. Motivation towards their studies may be a serious problem for some, and this may lead to anxiety and arguments between parents and their offspring.

The prospect of the future may be very daunting for some and at heart they may not be ready to give up the safety of childhood. Somehow it seems safer to remain focused in the present, so arguments based on the necessity of working hard for their future just make matters worse. Home education does take the pressure off young people to achieve at the same rate as their contemporaries, so if a young person has a problem of this kind there is always the option of postponing GCSE or looking at other types of qualification.

Another possibility that may be helpful is attendance at an evening class at college before the young person is 16. You can't insist on a place as the arrangement is at the discretion of the Principal, but most colleges are helpful. This may provide a way round the problem that 'he won't take it from me ... ' which is experienced by some parents, and it may make it easier to motivate a young person to study other subjects at home as well. Studying part-time at college may be an enriching experience for home educated young people as they would be working alongside people of all ages. It's also a way of finding out about the college environment, and it offers the young person the chance to become familiar with the world of further education before embarking on a full-time course. The parent has to pay the course fees but it may be possible to negotiate a reduction. The college may not have a policy for home educators so the request may be met with surprise, but it's always worth asking.

If the young person has had traumatic experiences at school and has started home education recently there will be a lot of sorting out to do. This may affect the timing of GCSE particularly when the young person's studies have suffered as a result. The student may have lost both confidence and motivation and may need to take a new look at the way forward. If examination courses have already been started it may be possible to carry on with them in some cases if the school is helpful and accommodating, but most candidates find that they have to start again from scratch. There is always the option of providing a general education at home for the last period of compulsory education, doing work experience once the young person has turned 15, and then applying to further education college to attend full-time in order to study for the exams. Full-time courses at age 16–19 are fully funded. GCSE doesn't have to be done at the same time as everyone else if the learner isn't ready for it, so don't despair if the young person leaves education without having taken the exams. They can always be taken later on and the motivation to succeed will be much better if the young person has a specific reason for taking them.

Be prepared for changes of plan. Their ideas for the future may change frequently and some of them may be totally unrealistic. Noelle says:

When she was 12 it was horses. She was determined to have her own stables and she was going to give her life to horses. Then it was basketball. She was really sporty for a while and she wanted to be a basketball star. She put a tremendous amount of effort into it. For a time there was something different every week and she tried on all these ideas like some girls try on clothes. It was a bit worrying as each new idea was definitely the real one, and she wanted to change her education each time to suit the latest plan. I know that teenagers change their minds a lot and they have to try things out, but I wasn't prepared for how stressful it would be for me. Now she's busy studying for GCSE and she wants to go to university. She still doesn't know what she wants to do but she's working towards the goal of higher education, which is such a relief.

Some of the ideas may seem unrealistic, but it's so important to respect the young person's hopes. Craig remembers:

When I was 13 all I wanted to do was to be a professional foot-baller. Nothing else seemed to be worth doing. When I look back now it makes me laugh! But my mum was great and she never made fun of me. She trucked me around the county to all different football clubs and she spent hours waiting in the car and washing the kit and listening to me going on about my dreams. She managed to keep me going with my education somehow although I remember being a real pain to her. I regret that. I'm glad she did, though, as I would never have got to college if she'd let me get away with it. I still play football sometimes, by the way, but I've got a life as well.

GCSE and home education

There is no minimum age for taking GCSE, and private candidates may take the exams when they feel ready to do so. Some young people take some subjects early. It's possible to spread out the GCSEs over several years, or take one or two first to test the system and find out any problems with entry. HEAS and EO will be able to give advice and information about taking exams.

Coursework often takes up an alarming amount of time and it's very important to get organized early. You can get exemplar material from previous years from the examining groups to help you to see what is involved, and it's useful to compare material from the different groups for the same subject.

Studying for GCSE

Some candidates use correspondence courses for some subjects and others employ a tutor to help them. Some students get the syllabus and a range of books and resources and simply work their way through the material, planning to complete particular sections of the syllabus by certain dates. This method is fine and many young people have gained top marks by studying on their own in this way. It's wise to include some flexibility in your schedule to allow for any delays or problems.

Learning how to make notes is essential. Make notes as you go through the material but be realistic. Don't attempt to write too much as it will become very burdensome and it won't help you to remember the key points. Note-making requires discipline so that you keep all notes up to date before you move on to another topic. Use colour, boxes round relevant sections and lists of bullet points to help you remember facts, formulae and vocabulary. Anything that helps you to remember is a good idea, including jokes and cartoons. Some people like to use mind mapping to organize ideas.

A surprising number of people don't have a clue about how to memorize facts. Here is one way of doing it. If you have facts to remember about certain topics, perhaps in history or geography, make a numbered list of the points. Identify a key word for each one and underline or highlight it in colour. Using your hands, associate each key word in order with one of your fingers and repeat them over and over again until the word is 'stuck' on your finger. Then repeat the whole of the point often, counting the point off on the relevant finger. This makes it much easier to recall facts and information in the exam. Make brief notes of facts and formulae on cards, shuffle them and ask friends and relatives to test you on the contents.

You should also allow plenty of time for revision and for doing past papers and timed exam questions. The marks allocated to each part of a question give invaluable guidance as to what your answer should include. If a question carries ten marks, don't be content with making two brief points in your answer. A question which is worth one mark would not need a detailed explanatory paragraph as this would waste time which should be spent on the rest of the paper. At present, studying past questions is very helpful as some of them may come up again in your exam in a very similar form. There are lots of revision guides on the market and there are sites on the internet which have revision material. These are not intended for initial study but they are useful for preparation as the exams draw near.

Make sure that you get mark schemes as they give very useful guidance on the content of the answers. The examining groups provide reports as well where the examiners give detailed comments on a range of candidates' answers. The IGCSE also provides standards booklets which give examples of actual scripts at different grades. These documents may be enlightening even if you are preparing for exams from another examining group.

When you get to the exam, it's crucial to read the paper carefully to see exactly what you have to do. Divide up your time between the questions and allow time for reading through the paper afterwards.

Don't be tempted to spend too long on one question or on one part of the paper. You can't get more than the maximum number of marks on any question, so it's better to make an attempt at each question even if you are short of time. Make sure you read the questions very carefully and think about their implications. It's all too easy to jump to conclusions when you are feeling under pressure, so take a deep breath and make sure you haven't made any silly mistakes. In questions that require calculations, be sure to show enough of your working to demonstrate to the examiner that you know the method just in case you get the answer wrong. Remember the invaluable three-point plan for getting top grades in exams:

1 READ the question.
2 SORT OUT the relevant facts.
3 USE the facts to ANSWER the question.

Too many candidates each year throw away marks by failing to answer the question that is being asked.

Post-16: the new national qualifications framework

A major change in qualifications for students over the age of 16 was introduced in England, Wales and Northern Ireland in September 2000. The new framework for qualifications is called Curriculum 2000 and it has been put in place to encourage young people to study a greater range of subjects and to give them the opportunity to combine academic and vocational study if they wish. The aim of the framework is to show how different qualifications relate to each other by grouping them into three types: general, vocational and occupational. GCSE and A levels are in the general group. Each of the three types of qualification has six levels; GCSE is at Level 2 and A level is at Level 3. The Qualifications and Curriculum Authority has drawn up a set of standards that qualifications must meet before they are accepted into the framework. Briefly, the main qualifications that meet the QCA's criteria are as follows.

Entry Level qualifications

Including the Associated Examining Board Achievement Tests, the OCR Certificate of Achievement, the RSA Accreditation for Life and Living and the Edexcel Entry Level Awards and others, these qualifications are intended to show basic competence in life skills, literacy and numeracy. If GCSE is not appropriate, the Entry Level Awards provide a means of giving young people some credit for their achievements that would be recognized by employers. The Entry Level Awards may also lead on to NVQ Level 1 and GNVQ Foundation

Level qualifications. There are tests at several levels of difficulty. It should be possible for home educated candidates to take these qualifications at a registered centre and further information may be obtained from the Examining Bodies who administer the awards.

National Vocational Qualifications (NVQ)

National Vocational Qualifications are in the occupational group and they are designed for people who are already in a job or in a work placement.

The qualifications are gained by assessment of skills in the workplace and there are five levels. Levels 2 and 3 are equivalent to GCSE and A level respectively. They provide evidence of skills and practical experience in a particular job, for example painting and decorating. NVQ Level 5 is designed to be equivalent to a university degree.

NVQs are often administered under Modern Apprenticeship schemes or as part of work-based training. These career choices enable young people to gain qualifications while they are working. They are run by local Learning and Skills Councils which replaced local Training and Enterprise Councils in April 2001. Details of NVQs may be obtained from further education colleges, the Careers Office or directly from the local Learning and Skills Councils.

General National Vocational Qualifications (GNVQ)

This vocational qualification may be gained in a range of work areas such as Health and Social Care, Engineering, Art and Design and Business Studies. The qualification is obtained by means of a taught course and work placements and it is available at Foundation and Intermediate levels. Formal entry qualifications are not normally required at Foundation level, but students entering at Intermediate level would need some GCSEs, NVQ Level 1 or GNVQ Foundation level. The advanced GNVQ has been abolished and replaced by Vocational A levels (AVCEs). Part One of the GNVQ will be replaced by the Vocational GCSE from Autumn 2002.

First and National Diplomas

These are vocational qualifications which are specific to certain skills such as floristry, childcare, greenkeeping, equine studies, fashion and textiles. They are administered by a range of providers including the Business and Technology Education Council (BTEC), City and Guilds and Edexcel. First and National are the two levels and they are designed to be equivalent to GCSE and A level. Study to GCSE level is required but specific entry qualifications are not usually needed for the First Diplomas. The Higher National Diploma (HND) is deemed to be equivalent to NVQ Level 4 which falls somewhere between A level and degree level.

New A levels

A levels are now combined into six units of which three are at AS (Advanced Subsidiary) level and three are at A2 level. AS level usually takes one year to complete and the A2 level is studied in the second year of the course to achieve the complete A level. Even if students don't study both years of the course to take the full A level their AS levels are intended to be qualifications in their own right. They are awarded grades, certificates and UCAS points for university entrance. Most AS and A levels will be assessed partly by coursework.

The Open College Network (OCN) also provides vocational courses from entry level to Level 3, and among the other specialist courses are the National Nursery Examination Board (NNEB) and Council for Awards in Children's Care and Education (CACHE) Diplomas in Nursery Nursing and Childcare.

Key Skills

The concept of 'Key Skills' was introduced as part of Curriculum 2000 and these consist of application of number, communication, information technology, improving learning and performance, problem-solving and working with others. Each Key Skill is available at levels 1–4 of the new national qualifications framework, and profiles are awarded to show what level the candidate has achieved for each unit. The first three Key Skills may be included as an integral part of full-time courses run by further education colleges and the intention is that all students should show competence in Key Skills. Students will be able to gain UCAS points for Key Skills which will be counted towards their totals for university entrance. It appears that so far both schools and universities have been cautious about the new qualification but in the future it may become mandatory for students for university entrance. The qualification is available to anyone over 16 in work, education or training.

National qualifications in Scotland

Scottish qualifications have been subject to some changes as well.

Standard Grade

This exam is taken by pupils in S4 in Scottish schools and it is assessed partly by coursework and partly by examination. It may be taken by external candidates at an examination centre. The Standard Grade is unaffected by the recent changes.

National Units and National Courses

These follow on from Standard Grade and they are usually taken by pupils in S5 at school. Highers have coursework and not all subjects are open to private candidates. The old Higher has been replaced by a new one which is divided into three units plus an exam. These make up a 'National Course' which has the same value as the old-style SCE Higher. Each unit counts as a 'National Unit' which is a qualification in its own right. Individual courses and units may be built up into Scottish Group Awards. By 2002 each of the National Qualifications will be available at up to five levels: Access, Intermediate 1, Intermediate 2, Higher and Advanced Higher. Advanced Higher has replaced the former Certificate of Sixth Year Studies (CSYS).

Other vocational and occupational qualifications provided by the Scottish Qualification Authority include the Higher National Certificate, the Higher National Diploma and the Scottish Vocational Qualifications. These are the Scottish equivalents of the HNC, HND and NVQ in England and Wales, and they have not been affected by the changes to the new Scottish qualifications structure.

Core Skills

These skills consist of Communication, Working with Others, Numeracy, Problem-Solving and Information Technology. Each candidate's Scottish Qualifications Certificate will include their Core Skills Profile and a certain level of Core Skills will be needed to qualify for a Scottish Group Award. Most Core Skills are covered through working on the different National Units so they will not be taught separately.

Leaving education at 16

Taking GCSE may not be appropriate for everyone and some young people prefer to go directly into employment. If there's an interest in a particular kind of work it may be possible to get into it without taking exams. Work-based training leading to a vocational qualification may be available. Sometimes if the young person is able to gain some relevant work experience while still in full-time education and is successful and reliable, this may lead directly to employment later. For example, many young people take on Saturday jobs in hairdressing salons, shops, stables, garages, garden centres, florists, hotels or other places. Some kinds of jobs are forbidden for under-16s including the collecting or sorting of rags or refuse, the delivery of fuel oils and the preparation of food. Thus supermarkets and food outlets aren't allowed to employ under-16s, but if the birthday falls early in the last year of schooling this may be a good option. No permission is needed for work outside of school hours, for example on Saturdays and during school holidays. The job may lead to full-time employment and the opportunity to combine it with an occupational or vocational course at FE College once the young person reaches the school leaving date.

As well as reading newspapers and watching the notice boards at the Careers Service and the Job Centre, it may help to take some active steps to find a job. Many young people have been successful in getting employment by writing letters to local firms giving brief details of their education, interests and any work experience. Potential employers may well be impressed by the young person's initiative, as well as by a well-prepared letter and CV.

Supporting young people as they grow up may bring its share of anxieties and dilemmas. Toni says:

> When our four children were young we worried about them all the time. We worried about their education and about their exams and we wanted them to have the very best. Our eldest boy in particular was a source of constant anxiety to us. He was very bright but completely unfocused, and he simply refused to do anything that we thought was worthy of his intelligence. But everything worked out in the end despite our fears and he had to do it in his own way. He's now very happy and he has a very good job with a finance company. Our children have their own futures and although it's hard not to be troubled about them, things tend to sort themselves out. Try not to worry.

CHAPTER 11

Some final reflections

What happens afterwards ?

The real test of home education is a simple one. What happens afterwards? Very little research has been done on the outcomes of home education in the UK, but what little there is has verified what we know from experience. In her book *Those Unschooled Minds: home-educated children grow up*, Dr Julie Webb (1999) follows up twenty young people who were taught at home. The stories are encouraging, positive and varied.

From time to time we hear news of young people who have left home education, either to go to school or to go into work or on to post-16 education or training. There are too many to quote here.

We might tell you of the boy who was withdrawn from school two years ago after being badly bullied. He is now happily settled in a new school of his choice, having regained his confidence and his ability to mix with others. We have had letters from families whose young people have worked hard at home and have gained good GCSE passes. There's also the young man who became severely school phobic after traumatic experiences in school and a break-up of his family. He struggled on at home for four years until the end of his compulsory education, and although his educational standard was low he found work in a local hotel. He soon settled into the job and found that he was happy doing all sorts of practical work and mixing with many different people. There are very many other accounts ... but we will content ourselves with two families' stories which show different but equally positive consequences of education at home.

Susan

Susan lived in a small village in a rural area of southern England with her son, Stephen. Stephen's early life had been happy and untroubled until his father died when the child was 9. From then on life became confused and frightening and Stephen became increasingly withdrawn. School became a problem as the other children teased him about his father's death. He began to have constant minor illnesses and he became lethargic and disturbed.

Matters came to a head when he started at secondary school and his behaviour immediately marked him out as a target for bullying. He endured the taunts and insults for some time before he began to run away from school. He would slip away after registration in the morning and hide until it was time to go home, and sometimes he would return home soaked and shivering as he had been out all day in the rain. Susan tried to solve the problem by appealing to the school for help, but neither the staff nor the education welfare officer seemed to be able to offer more than general advice. Susan remembers many occasions where the education welfare officer tried to get Stephen to go to school with her in her car, but he would break free and run indoors. After about a year the school began to lose patience and Susan was threatened with a school attendance order. Susan recalls:

It was at this point that I decided to take him out of school. He was nearly 13. By this time he was very disturbed and he couldn't have learned anything at school anyway. He was failing in every subject and he knew he'd never catch up. The only things that interested him were cars and motorbikes, and he learned a lot about them on his own. I discovered that I could get him to read by getting car manuals out of the library and eventually I got him to do some writing and drawing diagrams to do with cars and bikes. Anything that was a bit like school used to fill him with terror and he would go white.

I had a running battle with the education department as they sent an Adviser to check on Stephen's education and he said that I wasn't giving him a proper education. If they only knew how impossible it was for him to do any more! What he did was a big effort but they just dismissed it as not relevant. Stephen became completely phobic about visits from officials as he thought they were going to send him back to school, and I had to try to protect him from them. He would have severe stomach problems from the time that they wrote to say that they were coming until the visit was over. In the end I used to hide the letters.

I fixed up for him to go to my brother's garage on Saturdays to make the tea, run errands and to watch what was going on, and although it wasn't in school hours I had terrible trouble from the Adviser when he found out. I had to battle with them as they wanted to stop him going there, even though he wasn't breaking any rules and my brother wouldn't let him near anything dangerous.

It seemed like a lifetime until Stephen turned 16 and he was free. During that last year he got a bit more confident, especially when he began to realize that he wouldn't have to go to school ever again. He went to work for a local garage as soon as he could, and his passion for engines and mechanical things has helped him to overcome his reserve. Now he goes into work and laughs and jokes with the others, and you'd never guess what a terrified boy he was a year or so ago.

Lois

Lois educated her two daughters at home from the beginning. The early years led naturally into a relaxed, informal but rich educational experience which was full of art, craft, reading, play, visits and music. Looking back, Lois explains that the children's education was characterized by creativity, spontaneity and the use of the imagination:

> Very little education was planned as we were too busy living life and enjoying opportunities as they came along. When the girls were young they just played and played, and sometimes life seemed just like one glorious muddle. We believed in allowing natural development and we could see that they were bright, happy, imaginative children who had a real enthusiasm for many things. We used to meet other home educators and we did all sorts of things together, and we were always busy. I wondered what would happen as they grew older but it seemed wrong to interfere and to try to control the unfolding of their lives.
>
> Time went by, and both of our daughters underwent a change in their thirteenth year. Our older daughter became interested in maths and she began to study it seriously. Other subjects followed and later we enrolled her on some distance learning courses for exams. She achieved impressive results at GCSE and A level and she went to university to study Maths. She is now completing a higher degree.
>
> Our younger daughter became interested in music at an early age and she was able to spend as much time as she wished on her playing. Practice was always a natural and unforced part of life so we weren't really surprised when she decided that she wanted to take music seriously. GCSEs and A levels were needed for her application to music college, so we had to get organized and study for them. It wasn't always easy and sometimes we used to fight, but she succeeded. After gaining two A grades at A level she threw herself into preparation for the audition four months later.

She applied to two of the music colleges in London and was offered a place at both.

Naturally we are proud of their achievements but we've always placed greater importance on their development as sensitive and compassionate people. They have always made their own decisions and they have never been pushed. In fact, if an Inspector had descended upon us in those middle years it would have been very difficult to explain what we were doing in a way that would make sense to someone who was steeped in conventional education. But the outcome has shown that we were right to trust our instincts.

Towards the future

What still needs to be established about home education

Over the last one hundred years the amount of research published on education in school is truly phenomenal. The results seem to confirm that while you have one teacher and thirty or so children, methods which are similar to those used a century ago may still work best – in school.

There has been no large scale research into educating children at home. What we expect, when there is, is that the notion that there is a 'best practice' will be laid to rest. The constant debate in schools about the best method of teaching reading, maths or whatever does not make sense at home.

What strikes us about home education is the sheer variety of educational philosophies and approaches, all of which seem to work. We don't think that any one approach is likely to prove superior, but there is a need for some research into why different families use different approaches.

As we have shown, some families are very informal, allowing their children to learn through everyday experiences. More research is needed in order to find out how this happens in practice.

At home children learn to read at all ages, from 2 to 11 years of age. What determines this? More information is needed on 'late' readers at home and how most of them become highly competent readers very quickly.

Are dyslexic children better off at home simply because their parents can devote so much time to helping them?

How effective is home education? Most people want to see comparisons with children in school. A few studies have been carried out which tend to show that home educated children are at least two years ahead. But usually this research has been restricted to small groups of children who follow school-type programmes in the USA. Comparison, in fact, is very difficult. How would these children have done in school? Would they still have been two years ahead of their peers? What of children who are taken out of school and have a mixture of school and home education? What of children who have been taken out of school because they are school phobic or have experienced bullying? How can you find children in school with whom to compare them? The best way forward might be via a thoroughgoing study of adults who have been home educated.

School: a different view

Going further, is it possible that an insight into home education might make us look again at some of our assumptions about school? Most of us are so used to school that we think of it as a well-meaning institution at the very least, and we would not think of questioning its record on children's rights. But if you've been to the 'other country' of home education you begin to see school in a different light. We are not anti-school, but our experience of home education has made us aware of some of the failings that are inherent in our system of schooling. These shortcomings are not the fault of any individual, and they are such a fundamental part of the system that people tend to accept them without question. Let's take a closer look.

Take a typical everyday lesson. The teacher asks a question and the children who think they know the answer put up their hands. The teacher then accepts a right answer and moves on or, in the case of a wrong answer, asks another child. This is routine classroom practice. But what of all the other children who put up their hands? If they got it right they received no individual feedback. If they got it wrong they had no chance to engage the teacher in dialogue in order to improve their understanding. And this leaves out altogether those who didn't put up their hands in the first place. In the pre-school years children are able to ask questions of other people but once they begin school this natural and fundamental means of learning is taken away from them. What had been their right before starting school is no longer on offer, and the opportunity to ask questions becomes even rarer as they progress up the school and the teacher : pupil ratio becomes less favourable.

Here's another routine example. The teacher has given the class an exercise to do. The pupils can ask for help but the teacher can give only a very limited amount of time to each child. If the teacher were to do nothing else there would be time to spend about nine minutes a day with each child individually. In other words, although the child is supposed to be learning from an adult, he or she is in fact learning alone. There is no opportunity for genuine interaction.

We know of a home educated child who returned to school who kept asking the maths teacher for help when she didn't understand something. Obviously the teacher couldn't give her the attention that she needed. The girl was quite outspoken. They clashed. The head teacher talked to them both to resolve the situation. The teacher said he had 30 children to deal with and he could not give her special treatment. The girl said that she could not be expected to twiddle her thumbs because she could not proceed with her work. Impasse.

If children are in the process of learning they should be entitled to get help as and when they need it. Because we see these situations as normal school practice we don't think about the implications for children's rights. Similarly, pupils don't protest because it's how it's always been for them during their school career. Consider also the following examples:

- The amount of personal space that a child has in school would not be tolerated in any other working environment. Many children don't have their own desk or locker, and it's common for children to have to carry all their belongings about with them during the day.
- It's standard practice for schools to insist that children, especially younger ones, must go outside during breaks unless it's raining. Imagine the protest if tea break at work had to be spent in the car park!
- It's also quite possible that the number of hours spent working each week, including time for homework, contravenes the European Social Chapter on working hours. Teachers are demanding a 35-hour week while children in primary school are probably working nearly as many hours as this, and secondary school pupils are working greatly in excess of 35 hours per week later in their school career.
- Finally there's the question of unacceptable child–child interaction, some aspects of which would be arrestable offences for adults. A child can hit or harass another child almost with impunity. An adult who hits a colleague at work or who intimidates someone on the way home would be prosecuted for assault or for stalking. Of course such behaviour is not confined to children in school, but generally home educated children socialize when their parents are in the background. The parents may intervene discreetly or directly if necessary in order to nip such behaviour in the bud.

Why, we wonder, are children in school expected to tolerate conditions which would be unacceptable to adults?

Children's thoughts on their education

In a recent competition run by *The Guardian*, children in school were invited to describe 'The school I'd like'. The newspaper was swamped by 15,000 replies! The children's responses were classified into nine areas, three of which dealt with the school building and running the school. Although the young people were unaware of it, their responses in the other six areas describe the things that home educated children and their parents value so highly about home education.

A comfortable school [with] quiet rooms where we can chill out.

A safe school with bully alarms and someone to talk to about our problems.

A flexible school without rigid timetables or exams, without a one-size-fits-all curriculum, so we can follow our interests and spend more time on what we enjoy.

A relevant school where we learn through experience, experiments and exploration, with trips to historic sites.

A respectful school where teachers treat us as individuals, where children and adults can talk freely to each other, and our opinion matters.

A school without walls so we can go outside to learn, with animals to look after and wild gardens to explore.

These comments speak for themselves.

Finally, we must reiterate that our intention in comparing home with school is simply to emphasize that education at home has many advantages which may not be apparent to those who are unfamiliar with it. We have the greatest respect for the skills and expertise of teachers. But the experience of school is so deeply established in our culture that it's necessary to challenge some common assumptions about it, as our comparisons with home education have enabled us to do.

Postscript

As we have said throughout this book, home education is a valid option for parents to consider. No one can tell you whether or not it's right for you; the decision is yours. If you decide to give home education a try for a limited or for an extended period of time, it's unlikely that you will regret it. In addition, if you pass on what you have learned from the experience you will probably be contributing essential knowledge which will help to make a better all-round education for the children of the future.

References

Allen, W. (ed.) *National Geographic Magazine*. PO Box 19, Guildford, Surrey GU3 3BR.

Burton, H. (2000) *Menuhin*. London: Faber and Faber.

Davis, C. (1939) Results of self-selection of diets by young children. *Canadian Medical Association Journal*, September, 257.

Department for Education and Employment (2000) *Learning Journey: a parent's guide to the secondary school curriculum*. London: DfEE

Department for Education and Employment and Qualifications and Curriculum Authority (1999) *national curriculum Handbook for Secondary Teachers in England*. London: HMSO.

Donnelly, J. and Jenkins, E. (1999) *Science Teaching in Secondary Schools under the national curriculum*. Leeds: University of Leeds Centre for Policy Studies in Education.

Edwards, B. (1993) *Drawing on the Right Side of the Brain*. London: Harper-Collins.

Gear, J., McIntosh, A. and Squires, G. (1994) *Informal Learning in the Professions*. Hull: Department of Adult Education, University of Hull.

Home Education Advisory Service (2000) *The HEAS Maths Pack*. PO Box 98, Welwyn Garden City, Herts AL8 6AN.

Lewis, M., Feiring, C., McGuffoy, C. and Jaskir, J. (1994) Predicting psychopathology in six-year-olds from early social relations. *Child Development*, 55, 123-36.

Macaulay, D. (1998) *The New Way Things Work*. London: Dorling Kindersley.

McMillan, G. and Leslie, M. (1998) *The Early Intervention Handbook: intervention in literacy*. Education Department, City of Edinburgh Council.

Petrie, A., Windrass, G. and Thomas, A. (1999) *The Prevalence of Home Education in England: a feasibility study*. Report to the Department for Education and Employment, London.

Shaffer, D. (1993) *Developmental Psychology*. Belmont, California: Brooks/Cole Publishing Company.

Thomas, A. (2000) *Educating Children at Home*. London: Continuum.

Tizard, B. and Hughes, M. (1984) *Children Learning at Home and in School*. London: Fontana.

Webb, J. (1999) *Those Unschooled Minds: home-educated children grow up*. Nottingham: Educational Heretics Press.

Wood, D. (1988) *How Children Think and Learn*. Oxford: Blackwell.

Addresses and further reading

Home education: voluntary groups
Catholic Home-Schooling Network (CHSN)
39 Willingdon Road, Eastbourne, East Sussex BN21 1TN
Tel. 01323 725861
Informal network for Catholic families – newsletter, membership list.
Send SAE for details
Education Otherwise
PO Box 7420, London N9 9SG
Tel. 0870 730 0074
www.education-otherwise.org
Informal support network of home educators in the UK. Publications
include *School is Not Compulsory* and *Early Years*. Newsletter and
contact information

Home Education Advisory Service
PO Box 98, Welwyn Garden City, Herts AL8 6AN
Tel/fax 01707 371854
www.heas.org.uk
Support and advice for home educators throughout the UK.
Publications include *The Home Education Handbook* and *The Big Book
of Resource Ideas*. Magazine and contact information

Home Education Network
www.ie.embnet.org/hen/
email: hen@www.ie.embnet.org
Organization for mutual support in Ireland

The Home Service Organisation
48 Heaton Moor Road, Heaton Moor, Stockport SK4 4NX
Tel. 0161 432 3782
www.alphainfo.co.uk/homeservice/
Membership, newsletter and other resources for Christian home
educators

Islamic Home Schooling Advisory Network (IHSAN)
PO Box 30671, London E1 0TG
Tel. 020 7790 9981
Muslim home education support group

Schoolhouse Home Education Association
311 Perth Road, Dundee DD2 1LG
Tel. 0870 745 0968
www.schoolhouse.org.uk
Support and advice for home educators in Scotland

Other educational organizations
Education Now
Educational Heretics Press
113 Arundel Drive, Bramcote Hills, Nottingham NG9 3FQ
Tel. 0115 925 7261
www.gn.apc.org/educationnow and www.gn.apc.org./edheretics
Education Now is a research and publishing cooperative which
promotes new initiatives in educational practice.

Human Scale Education
96 Carlingcott, Bath BA2 8AW
Tel. 01275 332516
www.hse.org.uk
HSE promotes new educational ideas which encourage education in
human scale settings.

The following is a small selection of books on home education
Bendell, Jean (1987) *School's Out*. Bath: Ashgrove Press. A personal
   account of one family's experience of home education.
Dowty, Terri (ed.) (2000) *Free Range Education: how home education
   works*. Stroud: Hawthorn Press. Twenty families tell their own
   stories of home education.
Fortune-Wood, Jan (2001) *Doing It Their Way: home-based education
   and autonomous learning*. Nottingham, Educational Heretics Press.
   Based on 'the natural child, unschooling and non-coercion'.

Holt, John (1991) *Learning All the Time*. Liss, Hampshire: Lighthouse Books (in association with Education Now Publishing Cooperative Ltd., Derbyshire).

Holt, John (1991) *Teach Your Own*. Liss, Hampshire: Lighthouse Books.

Meighan, Roland (1997) *The Next Learning System: and why home schoolers are trailblazers*. Nottingham: Educational Heretics Press. Argues that home education is the system of the future.

Rose, Mary Ann and Stanbrook, Paul (2000) *Getting Started in Home Education*. Nottingham: Education Now Books. Advice on home education for beginners.

Thomas, Alan (2000) *Educating Children at Home*. London: Continuum. The first detailed research into methods used in home education with an emphasis on informal learning.

Webb, Julie (1999) *Those Unschooled Minds: home-educated children grow up*. Nottingham: Educational Heretics Press. Twenty adults who were home educated talk about their experiences.

A home education magazine

Choice in Education
PO Box 20284, London NW1 3WY
Tel. 020 7813 5907
www.choiceineducation.org.uk
An independent monthly magazine for home educators

Index

A level *see* Advanced level
Advanced level 96, 145, 146, 147, 152
Advanced Level, vocational 146
Advanced Subsidiary level 147
Adviser 46, 51, 53, 54, 134, 135
agriculture 85, 104
art 11, 32, 33, 40, 45, 49, 57, 65, 74–6,
    80, 85, 113–16, 137, 152
AS level *see* Advanced Subsidiary level
Asperger syndrome 137
astronomy 33, 48, 85, 99
autistic tendencies 137, 139
autonomous learning 51
AVCE *see* Advanced Level, Vocational

biology 97, 98
Braille 135, 139
BTEC *see* Business and Technology
    Education Council
bullying 3, 47, 136, 151, 154
Business and Technology Education
    Council 146

CACHE *see* Council for Awards in
    Children's Care and Education
Canadian Medical Association Journal, the
    (1939) 50
career, parent's 41
Careers Service, the 120, 141, 149
chemicals 66, 97, 98
chemistry 30, 96, 97, 98
Children Learning at Home and in School
    (Tizard & Hughes) 23, 28
children, number of home educated *see*
    number, home educated children
citizenship 57, 83, 85

City and Guilds 146
Cockerell, Sir Christopher 98
Code of Practice on the Identification and
    Assessment of Special Educational
    Needs 133
computer 13, 26, 27, 48, 49, 85, 93, 104,
    107, 109, 110
computer magazines *see* magazines,
    computer
computers 3, 40, 72, 86, 110
computers, familiarity with 57, 73–4
confidence 12, 14, 31, 65, 88, 91, 93, 96,
    97, 108, 112, 113, 127, 138, 142, 150
    of parent 4, 46, 92
conversation 21, 22, 23, 27, 28, 29, 30,
    42, 69, 91, 101, 123, 131
cooking 13, 33, 65, 72, 78, 80, 94, 111
Core Skills 148
correspondence courses 9, 45, 46, 48, 86,
    100, 143
Council for Awards in Children's Care
    and Education 147
County Music Service 118
coursework 16, 93, 99, 101, 109, 116,
    143, 147, 148

Dail, the 13
Davis, Dr Clara M. 50
Department for Education and
    Employment 33, 71
Department for Education and Skills 25
design and technology 57, 85, 110–13
DfEE *see* Department for Education and
    Employment
DfES *see* Department for Education and
    Skills

Down's syndrome 132
drama 9, 16, 44, 85, 92, 101, 117, 125
Drawing on the Right Side of the Brain
   (Betty Edwards) 76
Duke of Edinburgh's Award 129
dyslexia 88, 137
dyspraxia 134

ecology 98
Educating Children at Home (Alan
   Thomas) 34–5
Education Otherwise 2, 53, 54, 127, 143
education welfare officer 53, 138, 151
electronics 85, 110, 112
English 36, 44, 57–63, 69, 85, 87–92, 97,
   99, 103, 110, 137
environment
      child's 136
      learning 3, 23
      of home education 19
      school 12, 139
EO *see* Education Otherwise
European Social Chapter 155
examinations *see* exams
exams 17, 31, 47, 50, 84, 85, 87, 95, 97,
   100, 101, 106, 109, 119, 140, 141–9,
   152, 156
experiments 40, 66, 67, 96, 97–8, 156

flexischooling *see* part-time schooling
football 124, 128, 143
French 31, 48, 69, 100
friends
      children's 13, 40, 41, 45, 51, 73, 102,
         119, 121, 123, 124, 125, 128, 138
      family 97, 99, 100, 109, 111, 118
      parents' 4, 5, 38, 41, 49, 77
      teenagers' 125–6
further education college 49, 100, 111,
   119, 140

gardening 65, 78, 94
GCSE *see* General Certificate of
   Secondary Education
GCSE, Vocational *see* Vocational General
   Certificate of Education
General Certificate of Secondary
   Education 8, 9, 10, 21, 31, 32, 46, 48,
   84, 85, 87, 92, 93, 95, 98, 99, 100, 101,
   104, 105, 106, 109, 110, 111, 113, 116,
   119, 137, 140, 141, 142, 143–5, 146,

148, 150, 152
      and special educational needs 140
General National Vocational
   Qualifications 145, 146
geography 44, 47, 57, 70, 71, 85, 104–6,
   144
geology 25, 48, 85, 99, 105
German 42, 69
GNVQ *see* General National Vocational
   Qualifications
Guardian 156
gym 124, 128

HEAS *see* Home Education Advisory
   Service
Higher education 143
Higher National Certificate 148
Higher National Diploma 146, 148
history 44, 47, 57, 65, 69, 70, 71, 85, 96,
   101–4, 106, 112, 114, 115, 116, 117,
   144
HND *see* Higher National Diploma
Home Education Advisory Service 2, 53,
   54, 92, 97, 107, 127, 135, 143
homework 15, 16, 155
humanities 57, 69–72

ICT *see* information and communication
   technology
IGCSE *see* International General Certificate of Secondary Education
information and communication technology 57, 72, 85, 107
information technology 48, 74, 107–9,
   147, 148
International General Certificate of Secondary Education 99, 101, 144
internet, the 27, 72, 74, 81, 82, 85, 102,
   105, 107, 109, 144
investigations 93, 97, 99, 106

Japan 26, 27, 68
Job Centre 149
jobs 32, 149

key skills 147
key stages 55, 57, 83
knowledge, specialist 9, 12

languages 47, 57, 68–9, 85, 99–101
law 5–6, 44, 53, 86, 131, 135

LEA *see* local education authority
learning
  conversational 28
  formal 9, 31 *see also* structure
  informal 9, 13, 19–37, 44, 49, 94
  joint 12
  structured 29, 45–7
lessons 8, 9, 11, 12, 31, 42, 47, 78, 94, 117, 119
library 25, 26, 59, 63, 68, 72, 75, 89, 99, 100, 101, 102, 106, 107, 114, 151
libraries 4, 81, 99
listening 56, 58, 63, 76, 84, 91, 100, 101, 117
literacy 3, 25, 31, 37, 42, 50, 55, 57, 58, 145
Little House on the Prairie (Laura Ingalls Wilder) 71
local education authority 2, 4, 6, 42, 51, 53, 54, 55, 75, 133, 134, 135, 136
local group, starting a 127–30

magazines, computer 108, 109
marking 9, 14, 103–4
maths 12, 15, 24, 31, 32, 33, 34, 35, 36, 37, 42, 43, 47, 63–6, 88, 92–5, 97, 152, 155
Menuhin, Yehudi 42
mistakes 9, 14, 18, 74, 145
Mousehole Cat, The (Nicola Bayley) 71
museums 4, 70, 82, 101, 116, 128, 140
Museum, Victoria and Albert 116
music 30, 31, 32, 45, 47, 57, 76–8, 85, 87, 90, 115, 116–20, 152, 153

national curriculum 6, 9, 10, 41, 42, 43, 45, 47, 48, 55, 56, 57, 72, 83, 84, 87, 91, 93, 95, 97, 110
National Geographic magazine 40, 105
National Nursery Examination Board 147
National Qualifications, Scotland 147–8
National Vocational Qualifications 146, 147
New Way Things Work, The (David Macaulay) 72
NNEB *see* National Nursery Examination Board
Northern Ireland 145
number, home educated children 2
numeracy 3, 25, 31, 37, 42, 50, 55, 57, 145

nursery nursing and childcare 147
nursery school 22, 25
NVQ *see* National Vocational Qualifications

observation 29, 43, 66, 67, 79, 103
OCN *see* Open College Network
Office for Standards in Education 33
OFSTED *see* Office for Standards in Education
Open College Network 147
opposition 38

painting 74, 75, 112, 113, 115, 117, 146
Parliament, visiting 102
part-time courses 48
part-time schooling 6
Petrie et al. (1999) 2
philosophy, parents' 10
phonics 59, 60
physical education *see* sport
physics 97, 98
planning 9, 10, 32, 46, 48, 50, 78, 83, 111
playdough 40, 56, 75
playgroup 51
poems 11, 62, 64, 67, 73, 80, 102, 135
poetry 33, 44, 89, 90, 115, 116
politics 30, 102
post-16 qualifications 145
private candidates 106, 109, 111, 116, 119, 143, 148

qualifications of home educators 1, 5, 7, 8, 9
quizzes 43, 86, 102

reading 9, 14, 16, 24, 27, 30, 33, 42, 45, 56, 57, 58–60, 61, 63, 67, 71, 74, 81, 84, 88, 89, 90, 93, 97, 100, 103, 105, 137, 144, 152, 153
Record of Needs 131
religious education 57, 71, 85
revision 84
revision aids 100
revision guides 92
Robinson, W. Heath 72

school age 2, 20, 21, 24, 25, 37, 40, 56, 58
school phobia 3, 97, 138, 151
school refuser 27
science 27, 40, 42, 57, 66–7, 85, 96–9

Science and Technology Committee, House of Lords 98
Scotland 5, 41, 131, 147–8
SEN *see* special educational needs
social life 17, 41, 52, 121–30, 131, 132, 136, 140
social skills 121, 123, 127, 134, 136
special educational needs 3, 6, 131–40
specific learning difficulties 88
spelling 21, 91
sport 9, 16, 103, 104
Standard Grade 147, 148
statement of special educational needs 131, 133, 137, 138, 139
structure 21, 28, 32, 34, 37, 44, 45, 48, 70
Stuart, Morag 59
suicide 3
summer schools 119
Summerhill 32–3
swimming 11, 126, 128, 132, 136

teaching, structured 21, 28, 32
technology 3, 43, 72–3, 110–13
challenges 43, 72
teenagers 51, 85, 94, 118, 125, 143
telephone tree 129
television 21, 27, 56, 63, 70, 76, 96, 102, 118, 134

testing 14
Those Unschooled Minds: home-educated children grow up (Dr Julie Webb) 150
timetables 9, 11–12, 156
tutors 9, 46, 47, 93

UCAS *see* Universities and Colleges Admissions Service
UK *see* United Kingdom
United Kingdom 1, 2, 5, 6, 45, 93, 102, 129, 140, 150
university 27, 32, 143, 147, 152
Universities and Colleges Admissions Service 147

Victoria and Albert Museum, the 116
Vocational General Certificate of Education 146

word processor 73
workbooks 45, 62, 64, 88
worksheets 14, 42, 86
writing 32, 33, 42, 57, 60–3, 76, 81, 85, 88, 89, 90, 91, 102, 117, 135, 137
in school 14
written work 9, 14, 61, 88, 90–2